The Taste of Stories

The Taste of Stories

*Cornfields & olive groves:
A family heritage memoir cookbook*

by Jeanine Roche Calabria

Dedication

For my family, who has served as my inspiration and support through every stage of life and every chapter of writing this book – with love and gratitude.

For all those friends who I've cooked with or for, thank you for being my "raison d'être."

Table of Contents

Foreword 1
    My Mother's Pot Roast 4

1. Foundations

Moulin Roche 9
    Grand-Père's Salade avec Vinaigrette 13

Figs and Lemons 15
    Mom's Lemon Nut Bread 17
    Tangy Lemon Syrup 18
    Figs & Walnuts 19

The Hazards of Hair 21

Jeanine's Banana Birthday Cake 23
    Best Banana Birthday Cake 25

The Hoosier Capital Bake Off 26
    Chocolate Mother's Day Bonnet 29
    100-Year-Old Frosting 30

Pasty Rhymes with Nasty 33
    Cornish Pasties 36
    Jeanine's Pasties 39

Kitchen Traveling 43
    Belgian Endive au Gratin {Frances} 47
    Rosolli - Finnish Beetroot Salad {Katri} 49
    Finnish Birthday Cake {Katri} 51
    Anzac Biscuits {Mim} 55

Food as First Job Fallback 57
    Carrot Pineapple Cake Cream *61*
    Cream Cheese Frosting *62*
    Kahlua Chocolate Chip Torte *65*
    Kahlua Frosting *65*

2. From Courting to Newlyweds

Shipping Pies to Long Distance Lovers 69
    Banana Cream Pie *71*
    Pecan Pie *72*

How I Wooed My Husband with Cheesecake 75
    Rich New York-Style Cheesecake *79*
    Stuffed Acorn Squash *81*

Feigned Culinary Experience and the Sensual Art of Artichoke Eating 83
    Nanni's Fried Artichokes *85*

Smokin' Turkey 89
    Brined Turkey *91*

The Battle of the Rice Puddings 93
    Delia Benavide's Creamy Stove Top Rice Pudding *94*
    Rose Anderson's Custard-Style Baked Rice Pudding *95*

3. Raising Good Eaters:
The Culinarily Challenging Years

Channeling a Swedish Coffee Break 99
    Swedish Almond Torte *103*
    Vanilla Cream *104*
    Pepparkakor *107*

Nico's Fifth Birthday Party: A Public Soccer Disaster 109
    Chocolate Soccer Ball Cake *112*
    100-Year-Old Frosting *113*

Sucking the Belly of a Crayfish	115
Raspberry Drink (Hallonsaft)	*117*
Crying in the Yogurt	119
Homemade Yogurt	*121*
Peach Pie with Maya	123
Lattice Peach Pie	*127*
Chinese Chicken Salad	131
Chinese Chicken Salad	*135*
The Girl Scouts & The Rainbow Salad	137
Chopped Rainbow Salad	*141*
Sesame Dressing	*143*
Mom's Secret Brownies	145
Mom's Secret Brownies	*147*
Annette's Brownies	*149*
The Mother of a Wrestler	151
A Night at the Smoothie Factory	155
Calabria Smoothie Classics	*159*

4. Eating Green and Clean

Lime Jello and Swiss Chard on the Same Table	163
Cheesy Kale Chips	*167*
Raw Cheesy Dressing	*168*
Greens with Beans	*171*
Squeezing Grief In	173
Golden Broth	*177*

5. *Food for Good Times & Bad Times*

Life Lessons from My Freezer **180**
    Chicken Tortilla Freezer Soup...*186*
    Tropical Summer Bread *185*

Big Kitchen Cooking.. **189**
    Lauren's Sausage Gravy *191*
    Lauren's Biscuits..*192*
    Santa Fe Meatloaf *193*
    Meatloaf Glaze..*195*

Cheesecake Tragedy **197**
    Rich New York-Style Cheesecake...*201*

Carry-On Brisket **203**
    Diane Evan's Brisket *205*

Fanfare Food **207**
    Fruit Pizza...*211*

The Last Supper and a Toast.. **215**
    Calabria Antipasti...*219*
    Taralli with Anise *220*
    Zeppoles *223*
    Christmas Morning Popovers *227*

End of Garden Soup.. **231**
    End of Garden Soup *233*

Acknowledgments.. **235**

My parents' 1st bite as husband and wife,
March 17th, 1951

Foreword

Where do food memories come from?

For me, they all started with my father, ironically a man who never cooked. I best remember my father against the backdrop of a library. I still see him as a six-foot two-inch, dark, and intimidating man putting down his books to be checked out. "What is your library card number?" the stern and immaculately dressed gray-haired librarian asked him. "What is V-J Day?" my father countered with a booming voice that could be heard all over the quiet building. Without blinking an eye, she quietly responded, "Eight, fourteen, forty-five." I worried that maybe one night it would be a new librarian and she wouldn't know the answer, but it never happened. Instead, I saw two adults taking great delight in some friendly intellectual sparring.

Every Thursday night my father and I would make our library pilgrimage. Thursday night was also choir rehearsal night for my mother. This meant I had one-on-one time with my dad. It differed greatly from the times I offer my kids now, which usually involve food and they are the ones choosing the destination. But as a child, I soaked up these trips and realize now they were the foundation for a lifelong love of good stories. My father, Laurent Blankenship Roche, was intellectually gifted, well-read, and irritatingly opinionated. He was meticulous and consistent in his daily habits and had a worldview that often seemed at odds with the rural values of the community where he settled our family in Lebanon, Indiana. He prided himself on thinking outside the box and on remaining a big city Chicago boy in the middle of the cornfields of Indiana. Thankfully, he linked me to the world outside our safe little enclave. The books we read and the stories he told kept me very aware that someday I would leave my hometown and explore all those tableaus he had painted for me over the years. Many of the stories he told of his past revolved around the description of incredible dishes he had in the south of France while visiting his father's relatives and at home in Chicago where he grew up. My father never cooked, so it was up to my mother, sisters and me to recreate some of his fondly remembered recipes: tête de nègre, pineapple upside down cake and boeuf bourguignon. Never did our attempts match our target—his remembered version of the dish.

One story featured a Muscovy duck caught in the farmyard of his Tante Marguerite in Provence, whom he visited as a boy. Proud of his bilingualism, he showed us the recipe written in neat French handwriting. But this one we never attempted; it described how to catch, kill, and pluck the feathers from the duck before cooking. He also described in mouth-watering detail the rabbit stuffed with tiny black oil-soaked olives and braised with day-old uncorked Châteauneuf-du-Pape, the regional wine of his father's home. His food descriptions painted such beautiful, colorful culinary images that later I would study in France just to discover for myself what all the fuss was about. Yet never did any of the food I encountered there quite match the magnificence of his stories.

So what possessed me to think that now that I was an adult, it might be different when he came to visit me after my mother died? I wanted to present him with his favorite dish from my mother's repertoire, pot roast. I was so excited that I had thought to ask my mother for the recipe before she died. This recipe spills over five note cards. One lonely Sunday afternoon, when I had moved to California and was missing my mother's cooking, I called her up and copied it down. The process of writing it out was tedious; I should have taken heed that the dish would be too.

Nothing is at all straightforward. It was a mind-numbing process: the braising, then moistening the meat with water and rubbing in a dry powdery onion soup mix, then adding other ingredients every half hour or so during the two hours it cooked. However, the end product was worth the effort. My dad used to eat her version and say that it reminded him of the boeuf bourguignon he had in France.

I started the preparations for the meal a day before he came, because I remembered it was always better the second day. I couldn't wait to have him arrive with the earthy, scrumptious aroma wafting through the house. But when the time came and I served it to him with a big expectant smile on my face, he said nothing. Yet I knew that the dish tasted just like my Mom's because I grew up eating it on many a Sunday. I was left wondering if maybe the dish was so authentic that each mouthful poignantly conveyed the reality of my mother's absence. Or maybe once again it was that his memories of food were locked into an archetypal form that no one could possibly duplicate.

I brushed off the disappointment as I had the realization that these stories were really for the benefit of the storyteller and his audience. He never wanted to eat the whimsical dishes from his memories. If he had never told me these tales, though, I might not have understood how powerful food memories could be. Chasing down the source of his remembered dishes has made for some wonderful adventures in my life. Now I know that in fact sometimes the story itself is better than the dish, or at least as good as.

My Mother's Pot Roast

Yes, it's really worth it!

Ingredients:

Serves 6

- 2 ½ pounds beef chuck roast blade cut or boneless, cut into 1 ½-inch cubes
- 1 package wide egg noodles
- salt and pepper to taste
- ¼ cup flour
- 1 to 2 tablespoons olive oil, enough to just cover the bottom the pan
- 1 packet Lipton onion soup mix
- 4 ounces canned mushrooms, liquid included
- 1 teaspoon dry basil
- 2 to 3 dry bay leaves
- ½ cup Burgundy wine
- 4 to 6 medium-sized carrots
- 1 large yellow onion cut in 8 wedges
- 1 tablespoon barbecue sauce
- 1 teaspoon Worcestershire sauce

Directions:

1. Toss cubes of meat in flour and salt and pepper until lightly covered.
2. Brown the meat in oil in a large pot.
3. Add ¼ inch of water to the pan and simmer on medium high heat. Watch closely and when it begins to run dry, turn cubes of meat over and add another ¼ inch of water.
4. Let run dry again, then add onion soup packet, sprinkling it on top of the meat. Open the can of mushrooms and pour the liquid into the pot, being careful not to wash away the soup mix from the meat. Add the basil and bay leaf to the pot, then place mushrooms on top

of the meat. Pour the Burgundy wine around the sides. Fill the empty mushroom can with water and add this to the pot as well. The contents should be at about ¼ the height the pot.

5. Put the lid on and turn down the heat to simmer for 1 hour.
6. Meanwhile peel carrots and cut into 1-inch chunks; add to the pot after meat has cooked for 1 hour.
7. Add onion that has been cut in 8 wedges. Once veggies have been added, place in oven and bake for 30 to 45 minutes at 350°.
8. Prepare egg noodles by following instructions on the back of the package. Toss with a little butter to keep them from sticking together.
9. When pot roast is finished, add barbecue sauce and Worcestershire sauce to the juices and if necessary place in separate saucepan to cook down until thickened. Pour over the meat and veggies and serve over hot buttered noodles.

{ Me at age 2 in Lebanon, IN - where I spent my childhood }

1. Foundations

Grand-père (left) and comrade in arms, Laurent Pensa (right)

Moulin Roche

Every Sunday my grandfather, Grand-père as I called him, would make the salad for Sunday dinner. I saw him do it during family visits when I was a little girl. But the memory stands out in my mind because I thought it unusual that a man in my family would help with dinner. My dad never did unless a grill was involved. It wasn't like Grand-père just threw together some lettuce and tomatoes and put the bowl on the table, no. This took much more time and attention than that. First, there was an old, cracked wooden bowl that was used only for this purpose. He began by peeling fresh garlic and then placing the clove in the bowl along with coarse salt. He worked the salt and garlic into a paste with the back of a fork. He did this with a slow grinding force that would completely coat the entire salad bowl surface. He then added several tablespoons of olive oil and only a few drops of vinegar until he reached the right quantities of both. His vinaigrette was buttery more than acidic. Lastly, he would add the lettuce, often grown in the back yard. I remember being given the task of rinsing it with the hose and then spinning the water off as I twirled around and around with the French lettuce basket. Then he'd place the leaves in the bowl and turn them over and over with two large wooden tongs until each leaf was evenly coated with the vinaigrette. It seemed more a pleasant ritual than a household task. No matter who tried to make this salad, it never quite tasted the same as my grandfather's.

I wonder now if maybe he used the olive oil from his family's company, the Moulin Roche. It was a small olive oil shop owned by Grand-père's cousins in Orange, France. The shop sold nothing but olives, olive oil and containers involved in the selling and storage of these products. The ancient sign was made from an olive oil millstone hung on a metal arm over the front of the store. When I was fifteen, I visited this shop with my grandfather. He was researching a book on Alphonse Daudet, a Provençal French poet, and had invited me to come for the summer.

I had never flown on an airplane and my first flight was this one to join my grandparents in the South of France. I remember my grandmother telling my mother that I needed to be careful since she had recently heard that young college coeds were being kidnapped and sold into the white slavery rings that were prevalent in the Marseilles area. Who knows if these rumors were true, but I can tell you that I never took the sage advice of not talking to strangers more to heart. I flew from Indianapolis to Chicago to Luxembourg to Marseilles and made it safely without being approached by any strangers. I was young, naïve, and inexperienced both in traveling and in navigating big cities. I spoke very little French and learned quickly that I loved the exhilaration of being independent and traveling solo for the first time in my life. Of course, I was also scared to death.

So now, thirty-five years later, I wish I had remembered more about the shop and the people as I think about the quality of olive oil I use and the kind of cook I have become. That moment, meeting my olive oil-producing cousins, I knew was monumental. But I did not know why. I remember Grand-père's cousins crying when they saw him and how they looked at me with such amazement, like I was truly some kind of miracle. Grand-père had been the only one of the cousins to have children and so I represented a missing generation. When I tried to ask about why they didn't have children, I received an ambiguous answer about the war, starvation, and fertility.

This old man with kind blue eyes, identical to my Grand-père's, wanted to give me a present. He tried to offer me pretty bottles and baskets, but what I really wanted was a bottle of oil to bring back to my family. He found an empty bottle and filled it with their best, private stock oil. I tried it on a piece of bread that was pushed into my hand. It was like nothing I had ever tasted before. It was green-gold, pungent and almost raw tasting. I could taste "fresh." This was different from the shelf-stable oil that I was used to. Back home, my mother bought Mazola vegetable oil. I had never considered that oils had so many flavors and qualities. This was the beginning of a series of culinary "aha moments" I would have that summer. We took many pictures with Grand-père's cousins, their arms wrapped around me under the sign "Moulin Roche." Sadly, the store

no longer exists, nor do any of his cousins. My sisters and I are truly the last of the family line.

Later that day, Grand-père drove me up to the countryside where olive trees grew on the hill. When the road stopped, we parked the car and began walking the paths in between the trees. Every once in a while Grand-père would stop and look around; he was in search of something, but when I asked, he just put his finger to his mouth and his blue eyes sparkled as he beckoned me to follow him. Eventually we stopped and he pointed to a door built into the hill. It looked ancient and very out of place. I asked him what it was, and he turned and surveyed all the area around him and explained that these were the trees that produced the family olive oil. The doors were the coverings to the olive vats where the olives would be stored until the farmer could come and collect them with the cart to be taken to the press. He continued to explain that my Tante Marguerite, the woman who inspired my middle name, used to bring her Jewish neighbors here to hide them and keep them safe during the Occupation. I felt such awe, knowing that the woman I was named after had been that brave and I was literally witnessing history as I stood looking over the grove of trees.

Experiencing that kind of profundity at age fifteen was lasting. I knew that my family history would continue to influence my life. I vowed then that I would learn French and return so that I could speak with my cousins directly without the need for my grandfather's translation. I was young, energetic, and completely seduced by the South of France and the taste of olive oil. Now when I make salad, I try to remember this legacy, not taking the origins of the oil I use for granted and channeling just a bit of my Grand-père into the bowl.

Family farm in Caderousse

My dad's relatives on the family farm in Caderousse, 1950

The last of the Roche men (Top L. to R.) Dad, Grand-pere, cousin Gaby, cousin Pierre, Oncle Auguste, Caderousse, fr 1971

Grand-père's Salade avec Vinaigrette

Ingredients:

Serves 4 to 6
- 1 large garlic clove
- 3 tablespoons high-quality olive oil
- 1 ½ tablespoons red wine vinegar
- ½ teaspoon coarse sea salt
- freshly ground pepper
- ½ teaspoon Dijon mustard or 1 teaspoon fresh lemon juice (but not both)
- 1 head of fresh tender lettuce leaves

Directions:

1. Place garlic on the end of a fork and begin rubbing the interior of a wooden salad bowl with it.
2. Place salt in the bowl and use to help break down the garlic fibers while rubbing the garlic into the bowl.
3. Once well mashed, add olive oil, vinegar and optional mustard or lemon juice.
4. Add lettuce leaves and incorporate by tossing with dressing in the bowl.
5. Freshly grind pepper at the end and toss some more.

Lettuce leaves are best just picked from the garden.

Dad in his greenhouse

Figs and Lemons

My father carried on a complicated love affair during my childhood. It required him to build an attached greenhouse to our family home to accommodate his mistresses. These Mediterranean goddesses, both exotic and demanding, were fig and lemon trees. He loved them passionately. Every spring he would wheel these lovelies out of the greenhouse on a dolly and place them along the edge of the driveway, their sunny summer resting spot. I believe this love affair continued for many years until the fig tree stopped producing and the lemon tree succumbed to a bad case of spider mites. I feel fairly certain that we were the only family in Lebanon, Indiana that grew these fine botanical specimens, since friends of my parents would come over when they were blooming or bearing fruit and admire his kept women.

A transplant himself, I am not surprised my father nurtured these symbols of his beloved French past. My father loved all things from Provence. He was a botanist by training, but worked as a salesman for an industrial cutting tool company. The garden was his true passion. He would come home each night after work during the growing season, change into gardening clothes and disappear into the back yard until dinnertime. Though we all enjoyed the fruits and vegetables from his garden, no one else shared his passion for gardening, nor the required family car trips to view plant specimens. On those trips, he would inevitably launch into lectures with his captive audience that involved the use of botanical plants names. Frustrated, having no idea what he was going on about, I would break down and ask him the vernacular name of the plant he was discussing. Funny how later as I studied French in college, my father's insistence that I learn both the vernacular and botanical names assisted me in figuring out the meaning of many words.

We had to stay home most summers to water the garden or during the winter to check the temperature of the greenhouse for the very finicky orchids. The needs of the plants dictated the schedules of our lives. Irritating as this was, I now find myself with a lemon tree in my kitchen and am in awe with the appearance of each new fruit. I affectionately refer to the tree as "Dad."

A Meyer lemon from my tree

Mom's Lemon Nut Bread

Ingredients:

2 loaves
- ⅔ cup melted butter
- 2 ½ cups sugar
- 4 eggs lightly beaten
- ½ teaspoon almond extract
- 3 cups all-purpose flour
- 1 teaspoon salt
- 2 teaspoons baking powder
- 1 cup milk
- 2 teaspoons grated lemon rind
- 1 cup chopped pecans
- ½ cup chopped fresh cranberries (optional)

Directions:

1. Preheat oven to 325°. Grease and flour two loaf pans.
2. Beat together butter, sugar, eggs, and extract.
3. Alternate stirring in flour, salt and baking powder with milk.
4. Fold in lemon rind, pecans and optional fresh cranberries.
5. Divide batter into 2 prepared loaf pans (can also be made in mini-loaf pans).
6. Bake for 70 minutes. Cool for 15 minutes on a rack, then poke entire tops of loaves with toothpicks.
7. Slowly pour over poked loaves the tangy lemon syrup so that it runs down the holes and soaks into the bread.
8. Cool completely before removing from the pans. Loosen sides of bread before inverting onto a plate.

Tangy Lemon Syrup

Ingredients:
- ¼ cup sugar
- 6 tablespoons fresh lemon juice

Directions:
1. Stir vigorously until sugar is dissolved.
2. Pour over partially cooled loaves.

Figs & Walnuts

An Italian Christmas Tradition

Ingredients:
- 8 oz dried Turkish figs
- Walnuts in the shells

Directions:
1. Place on the table a bowl of figs and walnuts along with nutcracker and enjoy conversation with family while fitting pieces of walnuts into the center of a fig and popping into your mouth!

Me with hair restraints!

The Hazards of Hair

Spending time in the kitchen as a child leads to confident cooking as an adult. My mother knew this instinctively and never said no to my requests to try my hand at whatever she and my older sisters were doing in the kitchen. If I was interested, then she encouraged me to try. Having older sisters, I was always "mature for my age." I overheard my mother tell her friend on the phone. So, it was no wonder that at age six, I wanted to make my own birthday cake. By then, I was reading at a pretty high level and could definitely have handled instructions on the back of the Betty Crocker Cherry Chip cake mix. My mother granted me my wish. While she and my sister Susan were working on the rest of the birthday meal, I made my cake.

I had long, curly, golden hair, worn in two high pigtails on either side of my head held up with beaded pony-tail elastics. What I remember about the auspicious baking day is standing on the kitchen stool, happily dumping the mix into the bowl of the '70s mustard-colored stand-up electric mixer. I poured in the eggs and water and oil, and turned on the mixer. "Help me!" I remember yelling. The next thing that happened was my head being yanked down, closer and closer to the silver beaters, as one of my pigtails got wound around the beaters faster and faster. Susan, my seventeen-year-old sister, looked at me in horror. I remember thinking how slowly she moved. Then, as though she awoke from a nightmare, she screamed and yanked the cord out of the wall. By that point, my ear was in the batter, and I was quite stuck.

Over the next hour, my sister and mother unwound my pigtail, washed my hair, and baked my cake! I can't imagine baking it with all that potential for hair in the cake, but then again, that was my mother. She never wasted anything. Ever. I don't remember what happened when we ate the cake, whether we politely pulled out the hair from each mouthful, but what I do remember is still loving to bake and not having any trepidations about using the mixer.

Like me, my daughter Maya was making her own scrambled eggs at age five when she returned from morning kindergarten. She'd pull over the step stool and tie back her hair. I thought this was the normal way to raise children until we hired a thirteen-year-old neighbor to babysit; she was not allowed to touch the stove at her house and could not help Maya with dinner preparations. I realized then that our early cooking forays were not the norm. So, when I tell you there were a few cooking mishaps growing up, you'll understand that it all turned out in the end, but maybe a little more supervision is advisable.

Me telling stories, April 12th, 1967

Jeanine's Banana Birthday Cake

When I was growing up in Indiana in the 1960s, box cake mixes were at their height of popularity. I remember being asked, "Is this from a cake mix or is it from scratch?" Most people answered "box." Our family usually answered, "from scratch." This cake is a hybrid. I think my mother made the exception to the cake mix because my Aunt Bobbie sent her the recipe from her Missouri, Methodist Church cookbook.

As I grew up and my tastes became more sophisticated, I came to realize that true bakers didn't really use mixes, at least not the kind of baker I aspired to be. I spent years baking from scratch, weighing ingredients instead of measuring by volume to be more accurate. I made flourless cakes, almond meal cakes and even gluten-free cakes as health became more of my focus. But even knowing all that I do now about baking, if someone asked me what my favorite birthday cake was, it would be my mother's banana nut cake with whipped cream frosting.

I doubt many of my "foodie friends" would ever be tempted to make this cake if they read the ingredients list in a cookbook. But this is how childhood memories trump even trained palates. My mother making my birthday special, serving my favorite foods, honoring our mother-daughter love…all this I taste in one forkful of my birthday cake. My mother's frugality, a product of the Great Depression, shows up with her later addition of mini marshmallows in the whipped cream so that the frosting would last longer in the fridge. Originally, she just frosted it with whipped cream. But this only lasted for the evening; the next day the cake no longer looked appetizing. The mini marshmallows allow the cake to maintain a creamy frosting appearance longer.

When I was junior in college, I studied French in Strasbourg, France. For anyone who has ever spent a significant time in France, you know that excellent pastries of all kinds are never far away. In fact, the pastry is so incredible that you could never duplicate it in the U.S., nor could you much surpass the product anywhere in the world. So, when I tell you my mother sent me the ingredients for this birthday cake, worried that no one would have a cake for me, you'd know how special birthdays are in our family. I made the cake for my "French family", and they were quite surprised by the cake mix concept. Apparently, this trend had never made it big in France. I didn't tell Mom about my French cake…funny, but I can't even remember what that one was!

Me with birthday buddies, 1966

Best Banana Birthday Cake

Ingredients:
Serves 12

Cake:
- 1 yellow cake mix
- 2 eggs
- 1 cup buttermilk
- ¼ teaspoon salt
- 1 teaspoon baking soda
- 3 mashed ripe bananas
- ½ cup chopped walnuts

Frosting:
- 1 pint heavy/whipping cream
- ¼ cup sifted powdered sugar
- 1 teaspoon vanilla extract
- 2 cups mini marshmallows
- ½ cup toasted walnuts (optional)

Directions:

To make the cake:
1. Preheat the oven to 350°. Grease and flour 2 9-inch layer pans.
2. Mix all ingredients together, except nuts. Completely disregard all instructions on the back of the cake mix. Fold in nuts at the end.
3. Pour into 2 prepared pans. Bake for 25 to 35 minutes or until toothpick comes out clean.

To make the frosting:
1. Whip cream until stiff peaks form.
2. Fold in sifted powdered sugar, vanilla and mini-marshmallows.
3. Spread on top of one cake, then put second layer on top.
4. Frost top and sides of assembled cake with remaining frosting.

Optional: crown the top of the cake with chopped toasted walnuts

The Hoosier Capital Bake Off

I grew up in a small farming community of 10,000 people in central Indiana and was raised by parents who were from North Shore Chicago suburbs. So, most of my childhood I heard about how great it was to grow up in Chicago and how limited my local community was in respect to education and culinary offerings. I turned to cooking to drum up the excitement my local environs could not provide. My mother turned the kitchen over to me, simply requiring that I clean up and use ingredients that were on hand. In middle school I won the home economics award for making "Gnocchi Parisian." Most of my peers were raising animals, cheerleading, and playing basketball. I had a Siamese cat named Rama, no horse and spent time reading and playing board games with my family. I did run track, but mostly it was a way to keep my weight in check with all the baking I was doing.

So, it's not surprising that the proudest moment in my teens was winning the Hoosier Capital Cake Bake Off. I was in middle school and my mother was the leader of my Girl Scout troop. I decided to bake a Mother's Day Bonnet. The hat concept came from my sister's Barbie Cookbook from the 1960s. I used a couple of my mother's recipes from her files so that I could enter the "scratch" category.

As I think about it now, the cake was pretty challenging for a novice. The crown of the hat was baked in a small mixing bowl and the brim a large round layer pan all lined with greased and floured waxed paper. After the cake had cooled, I had to cut off the bubbles that rose while baking, and this would make frosting the chocolate cake with a creamy white buttercream frosting very challenging. Inevitably, dark crumbs would show through the frosting, and I would have to refrigerate the entire large cake and do a second frosting later. Often the batch of frosting would crystallize, and I'd be forced to make a second batch to keep the creamy smooth surface. I needed it to be uniform so that when I etched in the weave of a straw hat, it would look more realistic. I learned how to make mini yellow roses on a never-before-used rose tack and cut spearmint candy leaves as additional adornment. I added a real satin bow from my neighbor's florist shop inserted in the back.

The cake was lovely, and the recipe was fairly unique. Called "Pan-It Chocolate Cake," it was an unusual recipe mixed in the pan. It had no butter, but used oil, water, vinegar and baking soda, reminiscent of a science fair volcano. The dry ingredients would bubble up when the wet ingredients were mixed in. The frosting was called "100-Year-Old Frosting." Never again have I made a frosting quite like this one and wonder now if perhaps it was authentically historic. The end result is a perfect ratio of rich, creamy, and not-too-sweet frosting.

I made the cake three times: once for my troop bake-off, then for the regional, and finally for the state bake-off. Each time I became a little less frustrated as I understood how to deal with the idiosyncrasies of the recipes. Being featured not only in the Lebanon Reporter but also the Indianapolis Star was a huge deal.

As I think of my thirteen-year-old daughter's trip to China and all the activities she was involved in, I'm reminded that she lived in an extremely stimulating and sophisticated environment, rich in culture and variety. It's hard to believe that I was the same age when I won this award. Finding a way to express your teen angst is so essential to the adult you later become. It is usually messy, filled with much drama and gut-wrenching emotion. Mine was expressed through buttercream; I wonder how Maya will remember hers.

from the Lebanon Reporter - 1975

In honor of Maya's 13th birthday

Chocolate Mother's Day Bonnet

Ingredients:

Serves 12
- 3 cups cake flour
- 2 cups granulated sugar
- 5 tablespoons cocoa
- 1 teaspoon salt
- 2 teaspoons baking soda
- 2 tablespoons vanilla extract
- ⅔ cup vegetable oil
- 2 cups cold water
- 2 tablespoons apple cider vinegar

Directions:

1. Preheat oven to 350°. Grease 9-inch cake pan and a large metal mixing bowl and set aside.
2. Combine all ingredients and mix well for about 5 minutes.
3. Divide batter between greased pan and greased metal bowl. Bake cake pan for 30 to 40 minutes.
4. For hat top, baking will take longer due to the thickness. Be sure to check frequently by inserting a long wooden skewer until it comes out clean from the center, approximately 15 extra minutes of baking time.

100-Year-Old Frosting

Ingredients:
- ¾ cup granulated sugar
- ¼ cup flour
- pinch of salt
- ¾ cup cold whole milk
- 2 sticks unsalted butter, cut into small chips
- 1 teaspoon vanilla extract

Directions:
1. Mix together the sugar, flour and salt until well blended in a medium sized saucepan.
2. Stir in cold milk with a whisk and begin to heat at medium, whisking constantly.
3. Cook until thickened. Place pan in a large bowl filled with cold water and let stand for 30 minutes.
4. Using a rotary mixer, whip at high speed cooled frosting while gradually adding butter chips. Be sure to blend completely so that no lumps are visible before adding the next batch of chips. When all butter has been incorporated add 1 teaspoon of vanilla and blend.

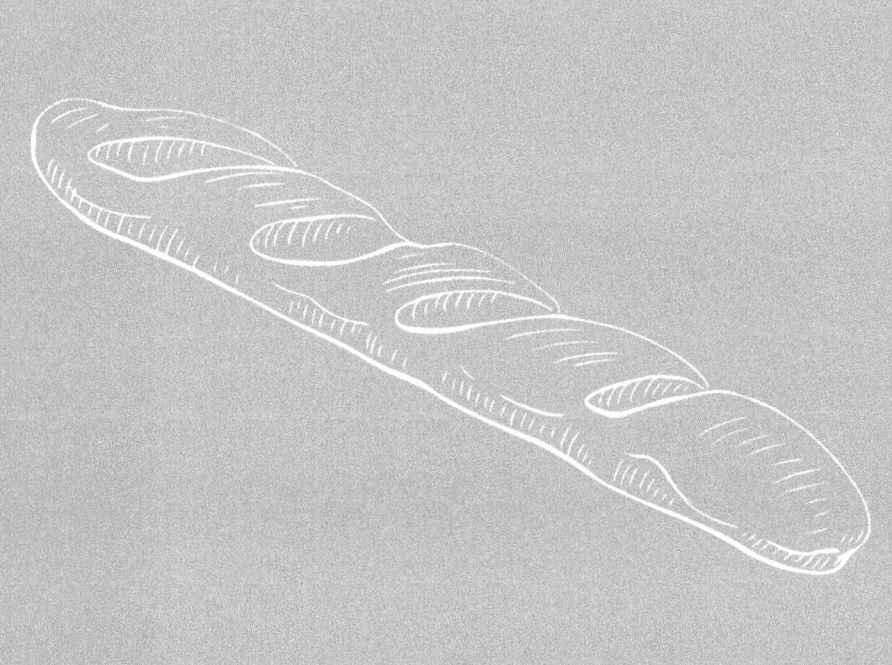

Pasty Rhymes with Nasty

Why did my Mom make pasties when they taste so bad? I don't know, because I didn't have a chance to ask her before she died. As I try to make sense of this cultural enigma, I discover many layers of possible meaning in the response. This meat and vegetable turnover was a mainstay for Cornish miners and is still eaten in English pubs and in the Upper Peninsula of Michigan where many Cornish miners settled in the late 1800s. Wrapped in pastry and loaded with dense root vegetables and tough meat, it tended to stay hot until lunchtime even in the dark and cold depths of a mine. But as a kid, the appeal of warm meat and root vegetables was lost on me. Besides, my mother's ancestry was Swedish.

What I remember about pasties growing up is loading mine with butter and ketchup to try to make them moist enough to swallow. So, one year during my teens, when my older sister Lauren suggested we give up an entire Saturday to make some for my mother's birthday, I balked. Guilt got the best of me though, since I knew how much Mom loved pasties. I showed up in our family kitchen at 7 a.m. in my orange fuzzy robe to start the arduous task. Why was our entire family set on making these things that weren't any good? Lauren, already covered in flour, smiled as she handed me a knife and pointed me toward the ingredients for the filling while she worked on the pastry. She talked about how she loved the flavor of the real butter that my mother only used for special occasions and how steaming the veggies in the pastry heighten the flavors of the vegetables. I couldn't stop thinking that my sister had lost her mind. Had she drunk the family Kool-Aid as well? I turned toward the mountain of onions, rutabagas, potatoes and flank steak and took a deep breath. Ever try to cut up a rutabaga? It's a lot like cutting into a rolling, waxed molten rock, dense on the outside and slippery in the inside, which makes the whole affair very likely to result in cutting off a digit. And in my mother's kitchen, every knife blade was dull. So, we ended up using serrated knives as saws, ironic since my father sold industrial cutting tools for a living. Miraculously, I kept all ten fingers.

My sister made the crust with Crisco, salt, unbleached white flour and ice water. This crust was the standard recipe in our home for fruit pies and quiches.

I found it very difficult to handle and have since opted for a recipe that uses half butter and half shortening and a flour water paste. Imagine trying to roll out this crumbly, dry pastry and filling it with cubes of vegetables that inevitably poke holes in the dough while transporting the pasties to a cookie sheet. Once safely settled on the pan, patches of dough were roughly applied with water to cover the damage. They weren't usually pretty when my mom made them, but Lauren had found cute farm animal cookie cutters and made steam holes using these. Once we baked the pasties and wrapped them in foil, we packed them in the old green Coleman cooler and drove to the surprise party for my mother at a nearby state park.

On the drive down, Lauren happily reminisced about our family vacations in the Upper Peninsula of Michigan. She reminded me of how we used to drive for hours following hand-printed pasty signs. When we would finally find a pasty stand, my parents would inquire about the contents of the pasties while we would sit in the car and cross our fingers that they were made with flank steak and rutabagas instead of hamburger and carrots. (Apparently, the authentic pasty recipe always called for flank steak and rutabaga.) Otherwise, my parents would leave the stand empty-handed, and we would be hungry, looking for some place to eat in the backwoods of the Upper Peninsula where dining options were very limited. Funny how siblings can have very different emotional responses to the same foods: Lauren remembered this fondly.

Once we arrived at the party, we got out of the car and announced the arrival of the food. My mother was touched that we had taken all that time to make her favorite dish. The September air was crisp and the pasties warm. I found my resistance melting a little as I held my pasty and warmed my cold hands. The rest of my family crooned over the meal. I shook my head in disbelief and fantasized about being Italian, willing my pasty into a calzone.

My mother was Swedish, but she prepared a 19th-century Cornish miner's dish during the 1970s in a small town in Indiana. Looking at her upbringing offered a few clues. My mother grew up during the Depression in a working-class family in an affluent suburb of Chicago, the child of Swedish immigrants. Never wasting food and economizing wherever possible was a lesson she learned during her childhood. She went to school with extremely wealthy kids from the North Shore elite. The discrepancy in income and class level always made my mother somewhat self-conscious of her origins. In her adult years, she saw this as a strength, the kind of muster that you would have to have if you were a pioneer living out on the Plains or in today's world a contestant on Survivor. So maybe that characteristic grit seemed to be present in the miners who carried pasties. Maybe they linked her to her ancestors and the act of making these dry, bland meat pies was a way of reminding her that she came from tough stock. So, she made the pastry, cut up the root vegetables and minced the cheapest cut of beef to be a part of that bygone era, a way of never forgetting or merely expressing a fondness for eating something from her childhood.

As I think of all the ways my mother has influenced my cooking, I consider the lessons learned from pasties. I have never made them again since the birthday assembly line with my sister, who still remembers them as delicious. But I learned that sometimes food just isn't about the end product. It can be about meaning far beyond the dish: it's the story of the origins; it's the time spent in solidarity in the kitchen; it's the wild search in the backwoods of Michigan.

Cornish Pasties

Ingredients:

Serves 8

Pastry Crust:
- 4 pie crusts (follow the recipe below or use your favorite pie crust recipe, doubled for 2 tops and 2 bottoms)
- 1 cup shortening (I use Crisco)
- ¾ cup chilled butter, cut into ½-inch cubes
- 4 ½ cups all-purpose flour
- 1 teaspoon salt
- 4 to 6 tablespoons chilled water

Pastry Filling:
- 1 medium rutabaga, peeled and diced into ½ inch (approximately 2 ¾ cups)
- 1 scant pound russet potatoes, peeled and diced in ½-inch cubes (approximately 2 ¾ cups)
- 1 large onion, diced
- 1 ½ pounds top sirloin, approximately 1 inch thick, cut into ¾-inch cubes.
- 1 teaspoon salt
- ½ teaspoon freshly ground black pepper
- 2 teaspoons water
- 3 to 4 tablespoons chilled butter

Directions:

To Make the Crust:
1. Put the flour and salt in the bowl of a food processor and pulse 5 to 6 times to mix the salt into flour.
2. Evenly distribute the chilled pieces of butter throughout the flour mixture, then pulse off and on until butter pieces are the size of peas.

3. Sprinkle 4 tablespoons of chilled water over the flour butter mixture and pulse a few times until, when gently pinched, the mixture holds together like soft dough. If it does not hold together, add more chilled water 1 tablespoon at a time, pulsing 2 to 3 times between water additions.
4. Put the dough in a gallon size plastic bag and press the dough into a ball by pressing on the outside of the bag and on all sides until a ball is forms.
5. Cut pieces of dough into 5-ounce pieces. There should be 8 to 9 small dough balls. Flatten each dough ball and place a piece of waxed paper between each flattened disc. Place stack of dough discs in the gallon bag and chill in refrigerator.

To Make the Filling:
1. Toss together vegetables (potato, onion and rutabaga) together with 2 teaspoons of water, salt and pepper.
2. Roll out the first disc of dough, on floured surface, to an approximate 9-inch circle. Place a mound of meat and vegetable on half of one side of the circle.
3. Using a pastry brush, moisten the perimeter of half the circle with water.
4. Dot the meat and vegetable mound with butter.
5. Gently lift and cover the meat and vegetable mound with the other half of the circle, then press the moistened edges together. Crimp edges to seal well.
6. Cut 3 vents into the top of the pasty and place on ungreased cookie sheet. Repeat the process until all discs of dough have been filled with the meat and vegetables.
7. Bake at 350° for approximately 50 minutes to 1 hour. Serve warm.

Jeanine's Pasties

With Wild Rice, Wild Salmon & Fennel

Ingredients:

Serves 8
- ½ cup wild rice, rinsed and steamed for 35 minutes or until soft
- 28 to 34 ounces frozen puffed pastry, thawed (approximately 2 packages)
- 1 ½ pounds of fresh wild salmon fillet, bones and skin removed
- 2 tablespoons butter
- 2 leeks, trimmed and roughly chopped in food processor (approximately 2 cups)
- 1 large carrot, roughly chopped in food processor
- 1 fennel bulb, trimmed and roughly chopped in food processor (approximately 2 cups), saving some fronds to decorate serving plate
- ¼ cup dry white wine or 1/8 cup Anisette or Pernod (licorice-flavored liqueur)
- ¼ cup freshly chopped parsley
- salt and pepper to taste
- egg wash (1 whole egg beaten with 1 teaspoon of water)

Serve with Creamy Dill and Cumber Sauce

Directions:
1. Melt butter in a large sauté pan. Sauté leeks, fennel and carrot for approximately 5 minutes.
2. Add ¼ cup dry white wine or 1/8 cup Pernod (Anisette) liqueur. Cook for 2 to 3 more minutes.
3. Season to taste with salt and finely ground black pepper.

4. Stir in cooked and drained wild rice and chopped parsley.
5. Depending on size of pastry sheets, figure out how to divide pastry to end up with 8 7-inch pastry circles, rolling out each sheet thin enough to arrive at the desired quantity.
6. Slice raw salmon into 8 even slices, removing silver skin and scales at the same time.
7. On half of the circle, place a layer of leek/rice mixture. Place salmon slice on top, fitting it to the pastry so that there will be a ½-inch border to seal sides.
8. Place egg in a small bowl and beat slightly with 1 teaspoon of water. Using a pastry brush, brush egg wash along outside edge of the circle.
9. Fold plain side of pastry over the filling and seal edges. Crimp decoratively to seal. Cut 3 small vents into top of pasty. Brush with remaining egg wash. Place on 2 cookie sheets that have been lined with parchment paper.
10. Bake pasties in a 350° oven for 35 minutes or until pastry is lightly brown.

I've altered these two pasty recipes so they are moist, the crust is easy to work with and you won't need a glass of water at the ready after every bite. I beg my family's forgiveness for having tampered with my mother's original recipe, but I believe the general public will be thankful. Second, I am including my own version of a pasty recipe that I came across while vacationing in Telkeetna, Alaska. The Alaskan miner's pasties were made with a pâté brisée and featured several different fillings. The one most appealing to me included wild-caught salmon, wild rice and a creamy dill and chive sauce. I learned through the server at the restaurant that the original pasties included folding half of the pasty over with a dessert filling of fruit and sugar—making the pasty a truly practical full-course meal in a pocket.

Me, Frances Verstraete, Dad - Indiana Dunes, 1980

Kitchen Traveling

By the age of fifteen, I knew I lived in a cultural desert. I would leave my little Indiana town and go as far away as possible. This set me apart from most of my friends. While they were planning trips to Raccoon Lake and Kings Island amusement park, I dreamed of visiting my relatives in France and Sweden. I was always on the lookout for ways to experience other cultures. To this end, senior year in high school, I convinced my parents to open our house to a complete stranger. Frances Verstraete, who lived with my family, was one of seven students from Youth for Understanding who attended my high school that year. She was as different from my sheltered, Midwestern persona as one could be. One of six children from an affluent Belgian family, she grew up speaking three languages and traveling during every school vacation to another country. She smoked, swore in many languages, and could look my father in the eye (she was six feet tall). She had no interest in cooking, but loved inviting over the other exchange students for dinner and had a talent for putting everyone at ease.

Inevitably, we'd end up in our kitchen trying to recreate foods that reminded them of home to waylay their homesickness. It didn't matter that the dishes seldom resembled what they ate at home. Most had never cooked before. It was a challenge to attempt dishes for the first time in a foreign country with limited access to the required exotic ingredients they were used to.

Miriam Chalk, or "Mim," was from Tasmania. She had curly gold-brown hair, freckles, and an incredible quick wit. She taught us that her country was founded by former British prisoners who had been sent there by the Royal Navy. I found this exotic beginning fascinating and wondered what kind of criminal ancestor she'd come from. She taught me how to make Anzac cookies, which required a trip to the Indianapolis Atlas Supermarket—made famous by David Letterman who used to bag groceries there. It was the only grocery store in the state that carried the Lyle's Golden Syrup that Mim insisted was an essential ingredient.

Katri Boyd came from a family who ran a horse farm specializing in harness racing with sulkies in rural Finland. She was slim and quiet, and you immediately knew how kind she was by her gentle approach to all that she did. She was by far the most proficient cook among us, and her two recipes, Rosolli and Chocolate Cake with Cream and Fruit, continue to appear on my holiday table. I loved that my mother was always willing to host one of these cultural cooking sessions and I feel fortunate to have kept the recipes from those times after all these years. Not all of the students left recipes with me, but they did leave indelible memories of their cultures.

    I remember, though, Frances insisting that French fries really originated in Belgium, and she would correct me if I didn't call them Belgian fries. Kees Schafrat, who was a Dutch visiting student, also came to these sessions but never brought recipes. Frances re-named him "Kase Kopf," which meant cheese head; apparently, the Dutch are known for the incredible cheese they make. The nickname never went over well with Kees, but I remember the two of them happily speaking their languages, pleased to feel at ease in their native tongues, Flemish being close enough to Dutch that they could understand each other. This was something I learned from them despite never having left my kitchen. I cultivated a cultural curiosity through those friends I made. It built my confidence to sit with others and listen intently as they tried to express themselves in another language and to be humbled by my own awkward attempts to speak in French—often their second or third foreign language. What I realize now was that I really used my kitchen to travel to the countries of my friends. I know that it cultivated a desire to continually explore culture through cuisine. I travel a little with them each time I cook one of these dishes in my kitchen.

Frances Verstraete, Exchange Student, 1981

Belgian Endive au Gratin {Frances}

Ingredients:

Serves 8
- 8 heads Belgian endive, trimmed
- 2 tablespoons butter
- 2 tablespoons all-purpose flour
- 1 cup milk
- 1 cup grated Gruyere cheese, divided
- 2 teaspoons grated Parmesan cheese
- ¼ teaspoon ground nutmeg, or amount to taste
- salt and ground black pepper to taste
- 8 slices thinly sliced prosciutto (or highest-quality ham)
- ¼ cup chopped fresh parsley

Directions:

1. Preheat oven to broil. Lightly grease a baking dish that will accommodate the endive.
2. Bring a large pot of lightly salted water to a boil over medium-high heat. Place the endives into the water. Cover, and cook until tender, approximately 10 minutes.
3. Place the butter into a saucepan, and melt over medium heat.
4. Whisk in the flour, and stir until the mixture becomes paste-like and golden brown.
5. Gradually whisk the milk into the flour mixture, whisking constantly until thick and smooth.
6. Stir in ¾ cup Gruyere cheese, Parmesan cheese, nutmeg, salt and pepper until well blended.
7. Cook gently over medium-low heat for 10 minutes, stirring frequently.
8. Drain the endives. Slice each endive in half from end to end.
9. Wrap each halved endive with a slice of ham, and place in the prepared baking dish, cut side down.
10. Pour the cheese sauce over the endives. Sprinkle with the remaining ¼ cup Gruyere cheese and parsley.
11. Broil the endive until cheese is golden brown and sauce bubbles, about 10 minutes.

Rosolli - Finnish Beetroot Salad {Katri}

Ingredients:

Serves 6

Salad:
- 1 small yellow onion, diced
- 1 big Granny Smith apple, peeled and cubed
- 2 small cooked potatoes, cubed
- 3 medium carrots, cubed
- 1 cup cooked beets, cubed (canned or boiled)

Topping:
- ½ cup heavy cream
- pinch of fine sea salt
- 1 teaspoon sugar
- 1 ½ teaspoon vinegar

Directions:
1. Layer each ingredient in an attractive glass bowl so that each color is distinct in the layering.
2. Mix gently the topping ingredients and "frost" the top of the salad.
3. Cover with plastic wrap and refrigerate until serving time.

No need to toss, this happens naturally with serving

Finnish Birthday Cake
{Katri}

Ingredients:

Serves 8 to 10

Cake:
- 6 eggs
- ¾ cup granulated sugar
- 2 teaspoons baking powder
- ½ cup all-purpose flour
- 4 tablespoons cocoa
- dash of salt

Topping:
- ½ pint whipping cream
- 1 teaspoon vanilla extract
- ¼ cup powdered sugar, sifted
- 3 bananas, sliced and tossed gently with the juice of one lemon
- 1 cup crushed pineapple, drained
- 1 cup sliced fresh strawberries
- ½ cup toasted sliced almonds

Directions:

To make the cake:
1. Preheat the oven to 350°. Line 2 9-inch cake pans with parchment paper; grease and flour pans, making sure to grease and flour sides, and set them aside.
2. Using a stand mixer with the whisk attachment, beat eggs and sugar until thick and foamy, about 5 minutes on medium high.
3. Sift flour, cocoa, baking powder and salt into a separate bowl.

4. By hand, gently fold dry ingredients into sugar and eggs, being sure to blend well but not flatten airiness of eggs.
5. Pour into greased cake pans.
6. Bake for 15 to 20 minutes. Cakes will appear dry on top and sides will begin to come away from the pan. Don't over bake!
7. Immediately slide a metal spatula around edge of pan to allow cake to stay intact and not crack during the cooling process. Cool completely.

To make the topping:
1. Whip the cream until stiff peaks form. Fold in vanilla and powdered sugar by hand.
2. Arrange 1 layer cake on serving plate and top with slices of fruit.
3. Cover fruit with the whipped cream. Repeat after placing second layer on top of cream.
4. Sprinkle toasted almonds on top of the whipped cream and place a beautiful slice of fruit decoratively on top.
5. Refrigerate until served.

Anzac Biscuits {Mim}

Ingredients:

Makes 3 dozen
- 2 cups all-purpose flour
- 2 cups rolled oats
- 2 cups sugar
- 1 cup shredded coconut
- 1 cup (2 sticks) unsalted butter
- 2 tablespoons Lyle's Golden Syrup
- ¾ teaspoon baking soda
- ¼ cup boiling water

Directions:

1. Preheat the oven to 350°. Line baking sheets with parchment paper, and set aside.
2. In a large bowl, combine flour, oats, sugar, and coconut. Set aside.
3. In a small saucepan over medium heat, melt butter with syrup. Dissolve baking soda in boiling water and add to butter mixture. Stir to combine. (Be careful; if the butter is hot, it will bubble up considerably.)
4. Add butter mixture to dry ingredients and stir to combine. Using a 1 ½ -inch ice-cream scoop, drop onto prepared baking sheets, about 2 inches apart (be sure to pack the scoop tightly so the mixture doesn't crumble). Flatten cookies slightly with the heel of your hand.
5. Bake until golden brown and firm but not hard, about 15 minutes. Transfer to wire racks to cool.

Find Lyle's Gold Syrup in specialty stores (product of Great Britain)

Food as First Job Fallback

The first year out of college is a real free fall for many. I certainly came down with a crash. It was the first time in my life that there wasn't the comforting structure of school and family. Although all this structure is invisible, the force it exerts on most of us is to pull us through challenges and come out on the other end with a degree in our hand and, for me, an unrealistic sense of worth. That isn't to say that I was worthless when I graduated from DePauw University with a bachelor's degree in French and International Business; I simply had an inflated view of my marketability. I thought that I had done all that I was supposed to do: graduated with honors, taken the Chamber of Commerce de Paris Business Exam, and chosen a marketable major. So, why wasn't I getting hired? Maybe because I didn't have a clue about what companies were looking for in an employee. I knew I wanted to use my French in a business setting, not in a classroom. In 1985 in Indianapolis, Indiana, that was quite a challenge. I believe there were only three companies at the time conducting business in French: Thompson, Kiwanis and at the boat import company., the company that ultimately hired me.

In retrospect, choosing a career in business was less a well-thought-out career path and more of a default. When it came time to choose a major at the end of my freshman year, I tried unsuccessfully to transfer to the Hyde Park Culinary Institute in New York. My father flat out refused to support this academic departure, believing a liberal arts degree was so much more valuable. Little did he know that I would spend a lifetime working in some food-related capacity and always feel that same yearning for my chef's degree. However, my father dangled the carrot of paying for a year abroad if I majored in French. Having a healthy dose of wanderlust and being what my French grandfather deemed "a parrot," I took the bait. I kissed my culinary career goodbye and packed my bags for France. The year of adventure, culture and language set me up for a lifetime of loving travel and learning about cultural and culinary distinctions.

When I returned to school, I knew that I didn't want to end up a French teacher, so I combined all my accumulated French credits from having studied abroad with political science and economics to end with an International Business concentration.

After my first year working in business, I knew that the degree I thought would lead to my marketability led to my misery. My first job was my worst job. While I waited for an interview, the partners were fighting within earshot. I heard them call for the chief admin while she was on the phone. Impatiently they screamed her name with several expletives until she humbly discontinued her call and came running. Stunned, I walked into my interview speechless and was offered the job for $10,000 a year. All too soon I would be summoned likewise by these intimidating bullies. Blinded by my determination to use my French and to prove that my choice in major hadn't been inutile, I plowed through six months of translating telexes, which required me to learn all the parts of a sailboat in both languages before I could contribute anything of value to the company. School had taught me this, how to persevere and jump through the toughest hoops, but in this scenario the reward had not been worth the effort. I had to work nights to pay my bills. Finally, my exasperation with the terrible work environment, which included having to stand at staff lunches and list my flaws in front of co-workers while the bosses either nodded their agreement or piled on a few more defects, led me to fine-tune my career objectives. Now I knew I didn't want to work in business using my French.

I started teaching ESL at night to Japanese businessmen and working at a French restaurant as a hostess to satisfy my craving for culture and creativity. I quit the job at International Resources, and quite promptly learned how to free-fall and land on my feet.

While working as a hostess at the French restaurant, I noticed how terrible their pastries were, clearly a frozen product. So, I learned how to self-promote, otherwise known as bullshit. I told the manager that I had worked in France as a pastry chef and if he needed anyone to improve the restaurant's dessert selection that I would be interested. I had actually learned a lot about cooking while staying with my cousin in Caderousse, France, a small farming village in Provence. I had also worked for a caterer and knew my way around a commercial kitchen. But I had never actually worked as a pastry chef in France. I had never even made the basics: pâté au choux, pastry cream and fondant. As a French major, I did pronounce the menu items more accurately than anyone else in the restaurant. Apparently, that was impressive enough, and I was hired on the spot. The very next night I found myself in the basement kitchen of the Common Market on the Circle making 1000 cream puff swans for the Annual Night Club Under the Stars event. I was happier than I had been since I'd left college. Finally, I had found my calling.

What I did not know was how furious the other chefs were at the restaurant. They saw me as an immediate threat to their superior professional experience. This healthy ego of most chefs is what keeps the industry such a competitive environment. When the restaurant manager introduced me to the rest of the all-male kitchen staff, I was like a lamb being led to slaughter. On my second day on the job, I reached into the walk-in cooler and pulled out the cream cheese frosting I had made the day before to complete the miniature carrot cake bites. Luckily, I tasted it before I started my work. I spit it out and couldn't believe it. My frosting had so much salt in it that it was inedible. I retraced my work from the day before as I started the second batch. I knew then that nowhere in the cooking sequence had I used salt since the butter was already salted. My frosting had been sabotaged! I pulled the manager aside and told him what I believed had happened. By the next day, he had figured out who was the culprit, and the guilty chef was fired.

Carrot Pineapple Cake

Ingredients:

Serves 12
- 3 cups flour
- 2 cups sugar
- 1 ½ teaspoons baking soda
- 2 teaspoons baking powder
- 1 teaspoon cinnamon
- 1 ½ teaspoons salt
- 3 eggs, beaten
- 1 ½ cups canola oil
- 2 teaspoons vanilla extract
- 1 8-ounce can crushed pineapple with juice
- 1 ½ cups chopped walnuts
- 2 cups loosely packed grated carrots
- 1 cup raisins

Directions:

1. Preheat oven to 325°. Butter and flour 2 9-inch layer pans.
2. In a large bowl, whisk together the flour, sugar, baking soda, baking powder, cinnamon and salt.
3. Add eggs, oil and vanilla and with an electric mixer, beat on medium speed for 3 minutes. Stir in pineapple and juice, nuts and carrots.
4. Pour into prepared pan and bake for 1 hour and 15 minutes or until cake tester comes out clean. Cool in pan 10 to 15 minutes and turn out onto rack to cool.

Cream Cheese Frosting

Ingredients:
- 1 16-ounce box confectioner's sugar
- 1 8-ounce package cream cheese, softened
- ½ cup butter, softened
- 1 teaspoon vanilla extract
- 1 cup chopped pecans

Directions:
1. Cream first four ingredients until well blended.
2. Frost top of one layer with frosting. Then place second cake on top and frost tops and sides of cakes. Sprinkle top of cake with chopped pecans.

Kahlua Chocolate Chip Torte

Ingredients:
Serves 10
- 3 large eggs
- 1 cup granulated sugar
- 2 cups graham cracker crumbs
- 1 teaspoon baking powder
- 2 tablespoons Kahlua
- 1 cup chopped walnuts
- 1 cup semisweet chocolate chips

Directions:
1. Preheat oven to 350°. Line a 9-inch springform pan with parchment paper. Grease both sides and bottom of pan and set aside.
2. In a mixer bowl, beat the eggs on medium speed and slowly add the sugar. Beat until light and fluffy. Add the graham cracker crumbs, the baking powder, and the Kahlua. Mix very well. Add chocolate chips and walnuts and blend thoroughly. Spread into the prepared pan.
3. Bake 25 to 30 minutes.
4. Cool on a cake rack. Remove sides of springform pan and parchment paper. Place on decorative plate and frost top with Kahlua Frosting.

Kahlua Frosting

Ingredients:
- 1 cup heavy cream
- 1 tablespoon sugar
- ¼ cup Kahlua

Directions:
1. Beat all ingredients together until soft peaks form.

Thanksgiving 1989 right after Carl popped the question

2. From Courting to Newlyweds

Shipping Pies to Long Distance Lovers

Falling in love brings out the domestic in me. I bake, sew, and cook for those I love. I grew up watching my mother do the same and vowed I would be different. But the truth is I become a baking fool for love. It started when my high school boyfriend delivered a dozen yellow roses to my door every Friday. He was the Mount Florist delivery boy. I loved yellow roses and he knew it. I would go weak in the knees each time the doorbell rang on Friday afternoon, and he'd be standing there beaming from behind the green florist paper. If my parents weren't looking, I would wrap my arms around him and the roses and kiss him passionately. He also knew that this Friday tradition resulted in my being beholden to him. I could have paid him with my virtue or in banana cream pies, and I not so naively understood that. So, we had this yellow exchange thing going that just drove me crazy for him…until I met my new boyfriend, Abraham Isaac Haq.

One weekend, I went to a college party in Bowling Green, Kentucky with my older sister Lauren. I first saw Abe leaning against the wall in the living room where twenty people were dressed like aardvarks, dancing to "Brick House." My sister was an interior design student and hung out with a very creative crowd. This beautiful man was watching me with such intense focus that I was unable to close my mouth as long as he stared at me. Tall, handsome, and built like a rock, with black curly hair that fell over his collar, he was Adonis incarnate. This Palestinian exchange student did not resemble one single specimen of the male population in Boone Country, Indiana where all my other limited romantic experiences had occurred. He was at Bowling Green State University on a track scholarship. In total, we knew each other for only six weeks. The distance between my home and his college campus was over 200 miles.

We had three weekends together and in between visits a lot of frustrating long distance phone calls that magnified the difficulty of the situation. Somewhere in the middle of our romance, I sent him a pecan pie. I used the recipe from my mother's Centenary United Methodist cookbook. It includes melted butter, dark brown sugar and loads of pecans. I used the ones that we kept in our freezer from my aunt's tree in Oklahoma. Every year after harvesting the pecans, my Aunt Barbara would put the nuts in a bag and run over them with the car. Then she would pack them up in this half-cracked state and ship them to my mother. It was one of those gifts that caused you to both smile and grimace. You knew that no sweeter pecan existed, but you had to do a lot of picking in order not to crack your tooth on an inadvertent shell caught in the groove of the nut.

The pie smelled heavenly just warm from the oven, and I packed it up just as soon as it was cool enough to handle, hoping that the same fragrant aroma would hit the recipient in the face when he opened it. This was long before bubble wrap and Styrofoam peanuts, so I had to be extremely innovative with designing packaging that would ensure the crust and glass pie plate not break during shipping. I wrapped it carefully in waxed paper and tied it up in several layers of newspaper. Using a utility knife, I custom-cut corrugated box parts to fit around the pie exactly so it wouldn't move during shipping. On the top, I simply wrote "To Abe, Love from your Rubin's study." (He had told me my bottom reminded him of a Rubin's painting.)

I could imagine his wickedly beautiful smile as he unwrapped the box and read the card. He would be surprised that I had remembered him telling me how much he loved a good pecan pie, and I knew that this was one good pecan pie. A week later, I received the chain that he always wore around his neck with his family crest on a gold medallion. He simply replied, "Loved the pie." I wondered if maybe he was part of some royal Arabian family, and dreamed of maybe someday having to wear a veil and live in the Middle East. I was planning my future already and had not even graduated from high school.

Our passion was intense and flammable, and it was surprising how quickly it was extinguished. One evening, he called urgently and asked me to immediately send his medallion back. I was crushed that his family's ire over his having given away the family jewels was more important than his feelings for me. Hurt, I wanted things returned to me, too.

I learned never to waste good baking on a long-distance lover. I couldn't request that he return the pie and all I had to show for my broken heart and lost virtue was the smell of burnt caramel each time we turned on the oven.

Eat the banana cream pie within 24 hours. The baked pecan pie can be frozen up to six months

Banana Cream Pie

Ingredients:

Serves 8
- 1 9-inch baked pie crust (prepared graham cracker crust can be substituted)
- ½ cup sugar
- 6 tablespoons flour
- ¼ teaspoon salt
- 2 ½ cups whole milk
- 2 egg yolks or 1 whole egg
- 1 tablespoon butter
- ½ teaspoon vanilla extract
- 3 ripe bananas
- ½ cup heavy cream

Directions:

1. Mix sugar, flour and salt in top of double boiler.
2. Gradually stir in milk and cook until thickened, stirring constantly.
3. Cover and cook 10 minutes.
4. Beat egg (or yolks) with a small amount of pudding mixture. Return egg mixture to the pot to become thick. Cook for 2 minutes more.
5. Remove from heat and add butter and extract. Cool.
6. Slice 2 bananas into baked shell. Pour cooled pudding mixture over bananas.
7. Chill for at least 1 hour. Spread top of pie with whipped cream and top with sliced bananas that have been mixed with a little lemon juice to prevent them from browning.

Pecan Pie

Ingredients:

Serves 8
- 1 9-inch unbaked pie crust in pie plate, with crimped edges
- 4 large eggs
- 1 cup light corn syrup
- ¾ cup dark brown sugar
- ⅓ cup butter, melted
- pinch of salt
- 1 teaspoon vanilla extract
- 1 cup chopped pecans
- ¾ cup pecan halves

Directions:

1. Preheat oven to 350°.
2. Beat eggs and next five ingredients at medium speed with an electric mixer until smooth.
3. Stir in chopped pecans; pour into crust. Arrange pecan halves on top.
4. Bake for 50 minutes, protecting edges with aluminum foil after 30 minutes to prevent excessive browning.

Off to company holiday party

How I Wooed My Husband with Cheesecake

I met Carl in 1985 on a blind date in Indianapolis. At the time, I was living in a communal housing situation with five roommates. One of the roommates was dating a colleague of Carl's and set us up. Having only just graduated from college a few months before, the idea of going out with a guy five years older who had a corporate job with a retirement package and benefits was a bit intimidating. When he called to invite me out, we had trouble finding a time. I was working three jobs, none with benefits: translating French nine to five, teaching ESL a couple nights a week, and working as a hostess on the weekends. The only free time I had was on Sunday. So, he invited me to see a modern dance troupe on a Sunday afternoon. I was so nervous that I decided to have him "checked out" before we left for the performance. I invited him for brunch with my five roommates. The poor guy probably felt like he was auditioning to be on The Dating Game.

When the day finally came, I was so anxious that I almost canceled. My roommate yelled from the second floor that some Italian guy with a black afro in a red Porsche 944 had just driven up in front of the house. Oh no, I remember thinking; my last boyfriend had a bicycle and worked as a courier, and I owned my grandfather's fifteen-year-old Ford Galaxy 500 that frequently needed to be towed home by my father. This was definitely not going to work. Besides, now I had to worry that in this neighborhood, he might have his hub caps stolen while eating brunch. To make matters worse, I served acorn squash stuffed with sautéed apples, onions and sausage. Little did I know, Carl hates all varieties of squash. However, he ate the entire serving and asked for seconds. Dessert was mini-cheesecakes. Carl loved them, requesting to take home all that remained from brunch.

The date was a success and a year later we were still seeing each other. So, for his thirtieth birthday I baked 200 mini cheesecakes so that I could spell out "Happy Birthday" on a large wooden plank, lit with mini candles. Five years later, we decided to marry and why not celebrate the big day with the same foods we had on that original blind date? My old roommates surprised us and served the now infamous stuffed acorn squash at the rehearsal dinner. They delighted in telling the story of how Carl ate every bite on that first date. Having almost snagged me, they couldn't convince him to take even a mouthful the second time around. But at the wedding reception, cheesecake in lieu of wedding cake was a huge hit. Neither of us got more than the one bite we fed each other, hearing later that his father had at least three pieces. Luckily, we froze the top and enjoyed the creamy bliss on our first anniversary.

Rich New York-Style Cheesecake

Ingredients:

Serves 12

Crust:
- 6 ½ ounces plain cookie crumbs (graham, chocolate wafers, ginger snaps)
- ½ cup plus 3 tablespoons unsalted butter, melted

Filling:
- 1 ½ pounds of cream cheese, softened
- 1 cup granulated sugar
- ¼ cup all-purpose flour
- 2 teaspoons grated lemon rind
- 4 eggs
- ⅔ cups sour cream

Directions:

To make the crust:
1. Process cookies for 15 seconds. Pour in melted butter and continue to process.
2. Press on bottom and sides of an 8-inch springform pan.

To make the filling:
1. 1. Preheat oven to 350°.
2. Beat cheese until smooth. Add sugar, flour, rind and beat again until smooth.
3. Add eggs, one at a time, then sour cream, beating after each addition.
4. Pour into prepared crust. Bake 1 hour in a water bath. Don't remove from oven when finished. Just turn off the heat and allow to cool completely in the oven.

I often bake ahead then "flash freeze" and cover with 2 layers of plastic wrap and then a box

Stuffed Acorn Squash

Ingredients:

Serves 4
- 1 acorn squash, halved and seeds scooped out
- 1 pound of ground breakfast sausage, browned and drained of fat
- 1 tart apple (I use Granny Smith), peeled, cored and coarsely chopped
- 1 teaspoon grated lemon zest
- 2 teaspoons fresh lemon juice
- 2 tablespoons melted butter, divided
- 3 tablespoons brown sugar
- 1 cup chopped walnuts
- 1 teaspoon cinnamon
- ½ teaspoon coarse salt
- 1/8 teaspoon cayenne pepper (optional)
- pinch of nutmeg

Directions:

1. Preheat oven to 400°.
2. Place squash cut side down in a baking dish. Pour in enough boiling water to reach a ½-inch depth. Bake for 20 minutes. Discard water and flip squash over to cut side up. Leave the oven on.
3. While squash is baking, combine chopped apple and browned sausage in a small bowl with 1 tablespoon of melted butter, the lemon juice, zest, walnuts and brown sugar.
4. In another small bowl, combine cinnamon, salt, cayenne and nutmeg.
5. Brush squash with remaining 1 tablespoon of butter and sprinkle with the cinnamon mixture to cover (you may not use it all). Fill the squash halves with the apple mixture and sprinkle with additional cinnamon mixture. Pour ½ cup water in the bottom of the baking dish (to prevent the juices that ooze out from burning and sticking).
6. Bake for 25 to 30 minutes, until the apples are tender and everything is golden brown. Cut each half in half and serve immediately, drizzled with any pan juices.

I've included this acorn squash recipe in case you want to seduce a potential suitor

Carl and I on a picnic in the park

Feigned Culinary Experience and the Sensual Art of Artichoke Eating

After our first date, I relaxed and found that I really liked Carl. To me his Porsche was no more than reliable transportation, but that he owned a mushroom brush and made fried artichokes, his Nana's recipe, was extremely impressive. Being in that newly-in-love stage when all you do is think about when you'll be together again, I wonder now if that was why it didn't seem strange to me that I never saw him cook again after the artichokes. I think he made me eggs a couple of times in the weeks to come and I saw a lot of soup cans in the garbage, but somehow I still was under the impression that I was dating an Italian lover and cook.

Clearly, I was blinded by infatuation. He was so happy to have me cook and entertain friends at his home or mine. He usually took care of the music and would arrange food artfully on the table, but spending time in the kitchen together was not becoming our gig. However, what I didn't know until I was already well into the relationship and had no plans of turning back was that Carl did not actually really cook anything besides eggs, artichokes and lasagna. What he knew how to cook was simply date-bait meals. They were pretty convincing, and, to this day, I still shake my head as I realize that I got reeled in by an electrical engineer who loves the fine design of good tools, not the act of actually using them in his kitchen.

"Nothing is really ours until we share it." -C.S. Lewis

Nanni's Fried Artichokes

Ingredients:

Serves 4
- 4 large artichokes, the size of a softball, rinsed and cleaned under cold water.
- ½ cup seasoned dry breadcrumbs
- ¼ cup high-quality olive oil, plus additional for drizzling on the tops -¼ cup fresh parsley, chopped fine
- garlic powder, salt and pepper to taste

Directions:

1. Cut the stems off flush with the bottom of the artichoke and reserve for later. Trim off the top ¼ of the artichoke with a sharp knife. This will remove most of the prickly tips. Using a kitchen shears, trim any remaining prickly tips around the periphery of the artichoke that were missed when cutting off the top.
2. To steam artichokes and stems, place all in a medium-sized pot. Fill with enough water to come up to half the side of the artichokes. Place cover on top of pot and steam for approximately 25 minutes (stems at about 15 minutes), until tender and a leaf can be easily plucked. They will be a drab olive color. You may need to remove the stems from the pot before the whole artichokes so as not to overcook them.
3. Remove artichokes from the pot and cool slightly. Using your fingers, spread the blossom wide open. Sprinkle with parsley, garlic powder, salt and pepper and breadcrumbs. The goal is to have the mixture go down into the blossom as far as possible.
4. In a medium-sized frying pan, heat 2 tablespoons of olive oil until glistening in the pan. Place 2 artichokes and all stems in the pan and brown the outside and bottoms of the artichokes, turning frequently to brown evenly. Remove the stems as soon as they are evenly brown. They will take less time. If needed, add a little more olive oil to the pan before browning the remaining 2 artichokes.

5. Place all artichokes and stems on a serving plate. Drizzle with remaining olive oil and serve. Have a "discarded leaf bowl" nearby.

How to eat an artichoke: Pluck a leaf from the artichoke, and scrape the soft fleshy part off the leaf by dragging it between your bottom and top front teeth. Toss the scraped leaf into a discarded leaf bowl and repeat until all the leaves have been plucked and scraped. Once you are down to the "heart" of the artichoke, cut in half with one side the tiny little leaves and the other the "bottom" of the choke. Discard the leaf half and eat the thick "bottom" half.

Smokin' Turkey

The year we got married, Carl and I bought our first house together. We were newly engaged and had found a house suitable for hosting our upcoming wedding. The house was located in the country on a five-acre lot that was part of an old beechwood grove. The majestic silvery trees would make a beautiful backdrop for an outdoor wedding. But on the day of the move, it was blisteringly cold, the roads snow-covered and treacherous, the trees laden with ice threatening to fall; not the most auspicious day to move in.

Determined to make the entrance to our new home cozy despite the weather, in the wee hours of the morning, I stole away to the house and started the makings of a scrumptious dinner. I wanted to thank our friends who were going to brave the cold to help us move in. What better way than to be greeted than with the aroma of a home-cooked dinner? I had been searching in my cookbooks for a dish that could bake all day and allow me to take it out of the oven just after that last piece of furniture was put in place. At this time of my life, I was so excited by the culinary work that I had been doing and finally having my own kitchen that I got caught up in the potential magic-making moment. Thinking about all the fantastic sides that I'd pull out, calculating the timing and how it would mesh with the move schedule became a preoccupation. The turkey stuffed with Italian sausage and cornbread recipe had been a siren song, calling me to attempt it.

I studied the menu and purchased the recommended cheesecloth to be draped over the turkey to keep the moisture in without burning the skin. The recipe suggested basting the turkey every thirty minutes by lifting the cheesecloth and replacing it after basting. Not being familiar with this way of cooking a turkey, I didn't understand that the cheesecloth needed to be soaked in water first and kept moist while roasting. The turkey also needed to be far away enough from the heating element, not touching it, but with such a large turkey it was a mere inch away. After carefully stuffing, basting, and covering the turkey with cheesecloth, I left the new house with the turkey happily roasting.

Many hours later, we had packed up the old house and loaded the truck in the freezing ice storm. Our friends got in their cars and caravanned slowly over with Carl and me leading the way in the U-Haul truck. When we arrived at the new house, nothing looked out of the ordinary, but we were greeted by a loud blaring siren from the house smoke alarms and in the distance we heard fire trucks. As we opened the doors to the front of the house, smoke, albeit fragrant with hickory, came billowing outside. Carl looked at me quizzically. I embarrassingly shrugged and said, "I thought it would be a nice surprise to have our first turkey in our new home today." I then went inside, opened the door of the oven, removed the turkey, and let it cool enough to scrape off the charred cheesecloth. Relieved that it was salvageable, I put it back in the oven nicely basted, ever hopeful to still have our first meal together in the new house. I turned to see our friends waving the firemen away, saying, "False alarm," and Carl on the phone ordering pizzas to be delivered pronto. Little did we know that our future marriage dynamic was so aptly played out during that one afternoon.

Brined Turkey

Ingredients:

Serves 10 to 12
- 2 gallons cold water
- 2 cups apple cider
- 2 cups packed brown sugar
- ¾ cup kosher salt
- 3 tablespoons tricolor peppercorns
- 5 whole bay leaves
- 5 cloves garlic, minced
- eel of 3 large oranges, cut into large strips
- 4 fresh rosemary sprigs, leaves stripped off
- 5 to 6 fresh sage leaves
- 5 to 6 sprigs of fresh thyme
- 1 uncooked fresh 15- to 20-pound turkey

Directions:

1. Bring to boil water, cider, sugar and salt.
2. Remove from heat and stir in spices, garlic, fruit and fresh herbs.
3. When completely cool, carefully pour over uncooked fresh turkey that has been placed in a plastic kitchen bag sitting in a rolling cooler. Be careful not to spill brine. This is much easier with two people. Close top of bag by tying off.
4. If possible, roll cooler outside on a covered porch where the temperature is below 40° or take out of the cooler and place in the refrigerator if you have room. The turkey needs to brine for about 16 to 24 hours.
5. When ready to cook, rinse off the turkey and pat dry. Prepare turkey per roasting instructions on the outside of the package. Brining reduces cooking time so watch thermometer carefully. Baste as usual with a mixture of turkey or chicken broth and 1 stick of melted butter.

{Leave the cheesecloth for cheese}

The Battle of the Rice Puddings

As I look back at my culinary road map, I see now how getting married and blending culinary traditions, even with a non-cook, really influences food preferences. I grew up loving my grandmother's rice pudding. I remember her coaching me through the recipe back in her Evanston, Illinois kitchen before a church pitch-in (the Midwest term for potluck). She always made it in her well-used avocado green casserole dish. The rich caramel smell of the brown sugar, egg, nutmeg and cream filled her little house with such a cozy aroma. It was baked in a water bath so the steam seemed to seep into every corner of her house, even covering up my grandfather's cigar smoke. To this day, the smell brings me right back to 1414 Ashland Avenue.

This dish was such a departure from my husband's family dish that he refused to eat it, saying, "That's not rice pudding." I stopped trying to convince him and instead learned his grandmother's recipe, which my entire family requests on special occasions. His grandmother made a simple version that includes slowly heating the pan with water and rice so that the rice would soften and absorb the milk fat once the milk was added. The original recipe didn't call for eggs, but instead allowed the pudding to simmer on the stove for hours until the rice, milk, sugar and cinnamon stick became thick enough to be called a pudding. Now though, we've added two eggs to quicken the thickening process toward the end. Never have I made this recipe without the pot boiling over a little bit. I've learned not to freak out but just wipe off the edge and lower the flame. Although I love this style too, I miss my grandmother's dish. I never make it anymore, fearful that I'll be eating the entire batch alone now that the next generation has learned that rice pudding is made on the stove top with cinnamon instead of nutmeg. I've included both recipes, though, and I'll let you choose which direction your culinary road map will go.

Delia Benavide's Creamy Stove Top Rice Pudding

Ingredients:

Serves 8
- 2 quarts milk
- 1 ¼ cup rice
- ¾ cup sugar
- 1 stick cinnamon
- 2 teaspoons vanilla extract
- 2 eggs beaten
- ¾ cup cream, whipped (optional)

Directions:

1. Soak rice in enough water to cover rice while heating the pot.
2. Add milk and bring to a boil, stirring constantly.
3. Lower heat and add cinnamon stick, simmering gently for 20 minutes.
4. Add sugar and vanilla and continue simmering. Always keep pot partially covered and stir occasionally.
5. When relatively thick and bubbling, remove lid and turn off heat.
6. Take 1 cup of pudding and add to eggs and stir. Add up to 3 cups pudding.
7. Return egg/pudding mixture to the pot and continue cooking for another 5 minutes.
8. Remove cinnamon stick and cool. If desired, whip cream and fold into pudding. Serve warm or chilled. Sprinkle with cinnamon if desired.

Rose Anderson's Custard-Style Baked Rice Pudding

Ingredients:

Serves 8
- ½ cup cooked rice
- 3 eggs
- 1/8 teaspoon salt
- 3 cups milk
- 1 teaspoon vanilla extract
- ½ cup brown sugar
- ⅔ cup raisins (optional)

Directions:

1. Mix above ingredients together and pour into a greased 2-quart casserole dish.
2. Set dish in a pan of water so that the water reaches halfway up the outside of the pudding dish, forming a water bath, and bake 1 hour to 1 hour and 15 minutes until set.
3. Sprinkle top of dish with grated fresh nutmeg and serve with a pitcher of half-and-half or whole milk.

In all the years that I've made Delia Benavides rice pudding, I've only twice added the cream, both times for holiday and special family events. Without the cream, the pudding is more of a Sunday night treat than something that I'd likely make for special occasions.

Maya stepping up in the kitchen - age 3

3. Raising Good Eaters:

The Culinarily Challenging Years

me and my Swedish Grandmother Rose, 1969

Channeling a Swedish Coffee Break

Over the Wabash and through the corn fields, to grandmother's house we go... It's not exactly as picturesque a route as the original song, but going to visit my grandparents felt adventurous nonetheless. There was always a sense of excitement when we packed up the car at our home in Lebanon, Indiana to head northwest on Interstate 65 to Evanston, Illinois, where my grandparents resided.

My father ran a tight ship when it came to car travel. His car was his office, and we were expected to abide by certain rules and keep our biological functions programmed to his announced schedule. No food in the car except for the lemon drops and Dentyne gum that he provided from his self-designed arm rest that also served as a car caddy. Wrappers were to be handed back to him immediately after popping the candy in our mouths.

Every trip started at 7:30 a.m. We traveled north on Interstate 65 for exactly two hours and stopped at the Rensselaer Inn to have what my parents called "Coffee And." Spilling out of the car with relief after being crammed into a confined space with my father smoking Winstons, the cold wind from the desolate fields slammed into my face, instantly invigorating me. As my father pumped the gas into his white boxy U.S.-made company car, we ran into the building laughing and holding our hair out of our eyes so we could see the entrance. Once seated in the dining room that overlooked the manmade lake, complete with pontoon boat and plastic wind toys, everyone ordered coffee and some kind of sweet. We rarely ate at restaurants and seldom ate sweets prepared by anyone but my mother at home. This was a major treat. I usually ordered something big, like a sticky bun covered in caramel and nuts or a cheese Danish or slice of pie.

As we nibbled our usually forbidden treats, my parents sipped slowly at their coffee. My father would inevitably strike up a conversation with the waitress about the area, noting things he saw as he drove in off the interstate that I had completely missed like the height of the corn or the demolition of an old barn. I loved the easy socializing and relaxed time that happened over "Coffee

And." I think was because it was something we all counted on, a deliberate break in the trip that interrupted the monotony of the otherwise flat, gray landscape of Northern Indiana. I had no idea that later in my life I would discover the Swedish version of "Coffee And" and wonder if we were actually just continuing the family tradition.

OK, everyone has coffee breaks, but "Coffee And" is different. It is more than running into Starbucks and running out with a latte. This is about the deliberateness of stopping the stream of work, taking time to relax and socialize and enjoy the steaming hot beverage and possibly the pastry, cookie or other treat that goes along with it. In Sweden it's called fika. I have two vivid fika memories while vising cousins in Dalakarlia.

Once, during my junior year abroad in France, I traveled via train to visit my Swedish cousins. It must have been in the fall because I remember my cousin's husband, Krister, harvesting the wheat from the fields. He came in every morning like clockwork for fika. My cousin, Anna-Karin, would have coffee ready and had either baked something or thawed out some cookies from her extensive bake goods collection in the freezer. Many of the recipes I copied down, and I still use the Swedish measuring tools that I bought at the time so I could reproduce them in the States. I was instantly reminded of "Coffee And" with my family. Krister didn't really come in just for a snack. He came in to pause his work, spend some companionable time with his wife and kids and then return well reinforced for the physical work that lay ahead with body and soul sated.

The second time I remember having fika was while hiking with another Swedish family in the Norwegian ski area called Idre in midsummer. Carl and I were hiking with our children in tow, then three, eight and ten. The path was steep, and we were feeling every inch of altitude gained with the weight of each of the children we carried on our backs. I couldn't believe it when my cousin Ake's wife Gunilla announced that it was time for fika. Was she a genie that could conjure up a coffee shop with just a rub of her thermos?

We stopped on the path with a beautiful vista of the valley below, and she spread out a blanket and proceeded to produce cups of hot cocoa for the children and coffee for the adults. She had brought with her Swedish cookies, fruit and cheese. We spent in total thirty minutes enjoying the place and food and each other. Gunilla is a schoolteacher, and when I thanked her for thinking ahead to provide such a nice spread, she seemed a little surprised that I thought this so special. She always did this on school trips as well with twenty-plus children in tow. Fika was an institution in Sweden, not something that could be eliminated from daily routine just because the surroundings changed. Who cares if you are away from the classroom or office? Fika must be carried on.

Kyle and Swedish cousins on Idre Fjall hike 2002

 I was reminded of how both my mother and grandmother, Rose Anderson, were very good bakers. They loved to share recipes and were proud of their baked goods. Although we had store-bought cookies in the house, making homemade baked goods was never thought a trivial endeavor. Everyone appreciated the effort it took and came to expect nothing less than homemade, especially when company came. The memory of having their cookies around a kitchen table with coffee is heartwarming even today. Never did I realize that I would live during a time that "skinny lattes with non-fat milk, no whip, no sugar" would replace the "Coffee And"/fika tradition. I long for that break with loved ones, baked goods and soul-filling memories. During my sons' high school years, I found tea to be an interesting substitution for fika. I would make a production of making a good cup, brewed from bulk tea sweetened with raw honey. This allowed me to insert myself unobtrusively into their lives for a few minutes while they took a break from homework and shared a companionable moment with me. Clearly, what's in the cup has less to do with the endeavor no matter what you call it.

 Here are some of my favorite recipes from my mother and grandmother's collections. I've also included recipes that I fell in love with in Sweden. I've converted the Swedish recipes to U.S. measurement, so don't be surprised by some of the unusual quantities.

Swedish Almond Torte

{Anna-Karin Andersson}

Ingredients:

Serves 8
- 6 egg whites, beaten stiff
- 1 cup granulated sugar
- 1 cup ground blanched almonds

Directions:

1. Preheat oven to 225°. Line 2 cookie sheets with parchment paper and draw an 8-inch-circle on each paper.
2. Beat egg whites and cream of tartar until frothy, then gradually add in sugar and continue beating until glossy stiff peaks form. (10 minutes)
3. Fold in almonds, being careful not to overmix.
4. Divide between 2 circles forming the layers.
5. Bake for 2 hours. Turn oven off and allow oven to become cool before removing layers. Don't open the door.
6. While the meringues are baking, start the vanilla cream. Cool completely before using.
7. Cool meringues completely on a wire rack before assembling the torte.

Vanilla Cream

Ingredients:
- ½ cup granulated sugar
- 1 vanilla bean, split and scraped (or 1 teaspoon vanilla extract)
- 2 cups whole milk
- ⅓ cup cornstarch
- 6 egg yolks
- 3 ½ tablespoons unsalted butter, softened and cut into 3 pats
- whipped cream and fresh berries (optional)

Directions:
1. Bring the milk and vanilla bean (pulp and pod) to a boil in a small saucepan over medium heat. Cover the pan, turn off the heat, and allow the milk to infuse for at least 10 minutes. Mix cornstarch and sugar together in a small bowl.
2. Whisk the yolks, sugar and cornstarch together in a heavy-bottomed medium saucepan. Place the pan on low heat and warm the egg mixture. . When the yolks are warm, gradually add the milk into the yolks in a steady stream. Stir constantly until thick and smooth.
3. Remove from heat and let the vanilla cream sit for 5 minutes. Whisk in the butter (and vanilla extract if you did not use the vanilla bean).
4. Cool completely by putting the pot in a sink filled with ice water. If not using immediately, cover with plastic wrap and store in the refrigerator until ready to use.
5. To assemble the torte, place one layer of the torte on a decorative cake plate. Then cover with ½ of the vanilla cream. Repeat. (If the vanilla cream has been refrigerated, it will need to be whipped with a mixer and a few drops of milk to become spreadable.)

Optional: top with whipped cream and toasted almonds and berries

Pepparkakor

Swedish Ginger Cookies

Ingredients:

Makes 2 dozen 3" cookies
- 1 stick of unsalted butter
- *¼ cup bacon fat
- 4 tablespoons of dark molasses
- 1 large egg
- 2 cups all-purpose flour
- 1 ½ teaspoons salt (flaked great!)
- 2 teaspoons baking soda
- 1 teaspoon ground cardamom
- 1 teaspoon ground cinnamon
- 1 ½ teaspoons ground ginger
- 1 teaspoon ground cloves (or allspice)
- 3/4 cup of light brown sugar

Directions:

1. Preheat oven to 350 degrees.
2. Place all ingredients in a food processor with a metal blade. Process well. Scrape sides of bowl and process again until all ingredients are incorporated.
3. Place dough on a piece of plastic wrap or foil and flatten into a disk. Wrap tightly and place in refrigerator for no less than 2 hours.
4. While dough is chilling, line cookie sheets with parchment paper. Put a cup of granulated sugar in a bowl to roll cookies in later.
5. Using a tablespoon, scoop well-chilled dough into balls and roll uniformly in sugar. Place on cookie sheets at least 2" apart and then flatten with the bottom of a glass that has been also dipped in granulated sugar in between each cookie flattening.
6. Bake in the oven for 10 minutes until brown. Let cool on baking sheet for a few minutes, then transfer to a baking rack to finish cooling.

The original recipe uses 3/4 cup of beacon grease. I like to use butter and add the grease for flavor but either way – the cookie turns out beautifully!

Channeling a Swedish Coffee Break

Nico's Fifth Birthday Party: A Public Soccer Disaster

With each of my children, one childhood birthday party really stands out. For Kyle, it was the pirate party complete with gold doubloons scattered on the sidewalk leading up to our house, and for Maya, it was her seven-year-old dress-up tea party. It was joyous to see little girls in pastel dresses running down the hill holding onto their sun hats to catch bubbles in the air. But for Nico's memorable party, it was a different story.

In July 1999, Nicolai celebrated his fifth birthday at the Indianapolis Kunz Soccer Stadium. I had just given birth to Maya and was exhausted from being up nights nursing. A soccer birthday party package looked very appealing. The stadium promised to provide everything from soup to nuts. Not only did they provide the entrance tickets for the professional soccer game but tokens to the concession booth and half-time entertainment too. At any price, it was a real bargain.

The night before the party, I had a pang of guilt. I had always put on the kids' birthday parties at home. At the least, I decided I could provide a homemade birthday cake. Naturally, I would attempt to make a soccer themed cake. I remembered the Mother's Day Bonnet cake from my youth. I remembered it always baked evenly and was also quite easy to unmold.

Miraculously, my recently widowed father, who had never baked a cake in his life, found the recipe in the old family recipe box, hidden in a cabinet behind my mother's baking supplies. Despite his macular degeneration, my father slowly read the recipe while I copied it down. The proportions seemed a little wacky, but I remembered as a kid that was one of the reasons I loved making the cake. It was fun like a sixth grade science project. So, despite my hesitancy in adding two tablespoons of baking soda and a quarter cup of vinegar, I went ahead.

The cake came out beautifully, just as I remembered it. Frosting it was very challenging, especially when it came to making the black hexagon patterns on a convex object. But the end result was very convincing; it looked like a life-size soccer ball sitting on a carpet of grass (green dyed coconut). My guilt assuaged, I packed the cake and my new baby into their respective carriers and headed to Nico's school.

My husband and I drove all the boys from Nico's kindergarten class to the stadium. The boisterous car ride over and lively stadium crowd made for a fun time. But now, exhausted just getting everyone to the party, I was thrilled that I wasn't trying to corral all that energy in our home. We arrived early and pulled together two long tables at the center of our party area near the concession stand. The boys ran around the tables and watched very little of the first half of the game. When it was time for their part in the half-time show, they marched out like little soldiers. Nico, who was born with one leg, stood at attention, crutches at his side, waiting for the star player to pass him the ball, which Nico kicked with his sole leg into the goal effortlessly. As a family, we were so used to Nico's disability, we often forgot that others seeing him for the first time were awed by his natural athletic ability. I was surprised to find myself tearing up as I saw the reaction of the crowd, who by then were all standing and applauding.

When the boys returned from the field, I unveiled Nico's surprise birthday cake. Even people in the stands were oohing and aahing. I felt conspicuous as I cut large pieces of cake and distributed it to Nico's friends. It looked yummy with all that creamy frosting and moist chocolate cake. But as each of the boys put forkfuls into their mouths their faces contorted. The envy of the crowd soon changed to horror as they witnessed each kid spit the cake out onto the artificial turf, crying, "Yuck!" and "Gross; what's in this cake?" Nico's face fell. "What's wrong with my cake?"

I grabbed his fork and took a bite. Horrors, it tasted cloyingly salty, much like Arm and Hammer toothpaste. I realized my mistake; my dad's eyesight had obviously gotten worse than I had thought. There was way too much baking soda in the cake. It was definitely inedible. But the frosting was so delicious. Incredulous, I tried several more bites because I just couldn't believe that the entire cake was so awful.

Then, as unsuspecting children lined up behind me hoping to get a piece of what remained of the cake, I hurried to the nearest trash barrel and dumped in the rest. It was so disappointing and humbling. My pride at once being the champion of the Hoosier Capital Bake Off was stripped by this flop. What started out being an easy party ended in complete disaster. A little girl from the stands came up to me and said reassuringly, "At least it looked really pretty." Despite my cake disaster, I pledge to you that it is a fantastic cake! Don't be afraid to try the corrected recipe because it really is one of those cakes you can always count on—as long as you don't triple the baking soda.

Assembling the Soccer Ball

1. Cover tray or plate that will be used for displaying the soccer ball with foil. Unmold cake from bowl by using a metal cake spatula to loosen the sides of the pan from the cake. Then turn the bowl upside down on top of the tray—tapping lightly on the bowl to assist with unmolding.
2. Place cake in the freezer for about an hour before frosting to keep crumbs from showing in the frosting.
3. Frost cake with the "100-Year-Old Frosting Recipe." Create a smooth surface.
4. Create from cardboard a 2-inch hexagon shape. Place the template on the frosting and use a wooden skewer to trace around the hexagon. Pick up the template and move around the cake until you have the approximate number of hexagons that resemble a soccer ball. Go back and use a tube of gel style decorative frosting to fill in the traced hexagons.
5. Finish by scattering flaked coconut that has been tinted with green food coloring around the foil-covered tray.

Chocolate Soccer Ball Cake

Ingredients:

Serves 12
- 3 cups cake flour
- 2 cups granulated sugar
- 5 tablespoons cocoa
- 1 teaspoon salt
- 2 teaspoons baking soda
- 2 tablespoons vanilla extract
- ⅔ cup vegetable oil
- 2 cups cold water
- 2 tablespoons apple cider vinegar

Directions:

1. Preheat oven to 350°. Grease and flour 9-inch cake pan and a large metal mixing bowl, then set aside.
2. Combine all ingredients and mix well for about five minutes.
3. Divide batter between greased pan and greased metal bowl. Bake cake pan for 30 to 40 minutes.
4. For soccer ball, baking will take longer due to the thickness. Be sure to check frequently by inserting a long wooden skewer until it comes out clean from the center, approximately 15 extra minutes of baking time.

100-Year-Old Frosting

Ingredients:
- 12 tablespoons granulated sugar
- ¼ cup flour
- pinch of salt
- ¾ cup cold whole milk
- 2 sticks unsalted butter cut into small chips
- 1 teaspoon vanilla extract

Directions:
- Mix the sugar, flour and salt until well blended in a medium sized saucepan.
- Stir in cold milk with a whisk and begin to heat at medium, whisking constantly.
- Cook until thickened. Place pan in a sink filled with cold water and let stand for 30 minutes.
- Using a rotary mixer, whip at high speed cooled frosting while gradually adding butter chips. Be sure to blend completely so that no lumps are visible before adding the next batch of chips. When all butter has been incorporated, add 1 teaspoon of vanilla and blend.

Sucking the Belly of a Crayfish

We were vacationing in a small Scandinavian ski community in the middle of July. My Swedish cousins had invited us after spending the previous summer in the States. After a beautiful day of hiking over lingonberry-covered paths and enjoying the fresh mountain air, we were invited to a special mountain dinner that my cousins had planned and prepared in our honor. Apparently mountain crayfish found only in high alpine streams were quite a delicacy and presumably quite expensive. The cousins had paid.

"No thank you," I stammered awkwardly when offered a second helping from the mile-high pile of boiled red crayfish staring back at me from the heap. There were so many left, and we'd barely made a dent. The faces of my eager-to-please relatives were fixed on our every movement, and the pressure to express our appreciation was never more palpable. I watched across the table as my son, Kyle, then ten years old, sat sucking the belly of a crayfish. "Mom," he said, "they're really good if you do this," and then he proceeded to slurp noisily, which seemed very intentional. There's nothing like giving a boy the chance to make gross noises at the dinner table. By this point, he had a pile of exoskeletons discarded in a heap next to him that he had worked through in less than fifteen minutes. I was pleased that I had raised at least one child to be an adventurous eater. In fact, not only was he adventurous, but he had also surpassed even me with his culinary risk-taking. He ate with gusto, and my Swedish cousins were shaking their heads in amazement, making that distinctively Swedish sound, "ya ha."

The family honor was on the line if we didn't carefully handle this delicate culinary situation. Thank God for Kyle, since my husband had gone a bit green around the gills while pushing legs and claws around on his plate. The fishy smell clearly nauseated him. The other two kids were so young that their feet didn't even reach the floor from their seats. They were happily sucking on rusks, Swedish hardtack and slurping on hallonsaft, homemade raspberry juice, oblivious to the predicament at hand. Kyle was taking one for the team, and I had best change my "no thank you" to "on second thought, please pass me five more."

The steamed mountain crayfish recipe does not appear, as I've never attempted to make them at home, but saft is a real favorite and takes less courage to both make and drink!

Raspberry Drink (Hallonsaft)

Ingredients:

Makes 3 quarts concentrate
- 2 quarts fresh and cleaned raspberries (or strawberries), stems and hulls removed
- 2 quarts water
- 4. ½ cups granulated sugar
- 4 teaspoons citric acid (available where canning supplies are sold, typically at hardware stores in the summer)

Directions:

1. Simmer berries until the fruit dissolves, about 20 minutes. Be careful not to let boil over.
2. Then pour contents over a large bowl covered with cheesecloth to strain out remaining fruit and capture the juice. You can also use a fine mesh strainer if you have one. Press fruit gently to release extra juice, but don't allow pureed fruit to pass through, as it will make the saft cloudy.
3. Add granulated sugar and citric acid. Mix until completely dissolved. Taste for desired sweetness and add more sugar if it's still too tart for your taste. Cool completely.
4. At this point, you can freeze the saft for later use.
5. To serve, pour ¼ cup of saft into a glass. Dilute with cold water or seltzer to desired strength and add ice.
6. Optional: add squeezed fresh lime juice and/or a slice of lime.

In Sweden, the winters are dark and harsh and the summers swift and sweet. No wonder everyone is into berry picking. By processing all those summer raspberries into a syrup, they can be enjoyed year round. Saft is basically a raspberry syrup concentrate that you dilute to drink like juice or added to other beverages as a tart complement.

Never too young to help out in the kitchen, 2003

Crying in the Yogurt

It was a Friday night and Maya and I were home alone. I suggested watching a movie together and she said, "Hey, how about we try out your new yogurt maker?" I was thrilled that my eight-year-old daughter wanted to spend time with me in the kitchen.

As we prepared for yogurt production, we talked about her afternoon at soccer. We walked around the room reading the ingredient list and preparing our utensils. Maya's curly brown ponytail bobbed from side to side as she pulled out equipment and continued to relay information as I listened distractedly. From time to time, she asked me questions about what I was doing. She wanted to know why temperature is so important and what "yogurt starter" is. She poured a half gallon of organic milk into a large pot, and I raised the temperature to bring it to a boil. We both watched carefully so that the milk didn't boil over. Once we arrived at 125 degrees, I whisked away the pot from the stove and set it into a sink already filled with cool water. Maya carefully clipped the thermometer onto the rim of the pot. She sat down at a stool and waited for it to cool. Her slight frame seemed limp and her expression a little distracted.

As suddenly as the milk came to a boil, a flood of emotion spilled out from her formerly calm face. She blurted out that she felt excluded both on the soccer field and off. Instinctively, I went over and hugged her. My embrace was an invitation to open the floodgates and let the tears flow. She cried and cried, and I hugged and hugged. Had we been sitting in front of the television literally "plugged in" ourselves, I venture to guess that this moment would never have happened.

Yogurt is smooth, creamy and nourishing. Learning how to make it requires paying attention to subtleties. It is about heating the water to exact temperatures, transitioning ingredients from heat to steam, and respecting the relationship of living organisms needing a delicate balance of warmth and humidity to survive. The correlation with my parenting and yogurt making was a profound one for me. Pay attention to the temperature, not overheating or underheating. If the milk is too hot when you add the starter, the yogurt won't set up and the consistency will be watery. If the milk cools too much, the bacteria won't be activated. Hold daughter at just the moment when tears pool on the edges of her dark brown eyes, squeeze gently and stroke her back. Warm energy transferred from mother to daughter allows the negative energy to escape, allowing for nourishment to replace it. Make space, allow time for tears, talk and love. Create space in your life and make yogurt.

After a good night's sleep, things seemed better in the morning. We excitedly pulled the yogurt out of its watery nest and spooned some into dishes. We dug in and puckered up in response to the sour yogurt. "No problem," I quipped, "we will just add some of the homemade raspberry jam that you and Lydia made this summer." We dug in again to the now pink yogurt, but it was still so sour we could feel the taste buds at the backs of our mouths contract in response. Maya added granola and I just toughed it out.

That night Maya went to soccer practice and not much had changed. The situation continued to be difficult, but somehow she seemed fortified to carry on. Raspberry jam or not, some things in life are tough to swallow; we either learn how to sweeten them or choose to stop eating them entirely.

Homemade Yogurt

Ingredients:
Makes 2 liters
- 1 packet yogurt starter
  (I recommend "Sweet (Y5)" from the New England Cheesemaking Supply Company in Deerfield, MA. (www.cheesemaking.com)
- 2 liters fresh, raw, whole milk
- Yogourmet Yogurt Maker (or other yogurt maker)
- High-quality digital thermometer

Directions:
1. 1. Follow the directions from your yogurt maker to make the yogurt.

I learned about the nutritional importance of making pure yogurt without any gelatin or other fillers from a nutritional training program. Though it takes some getting used to the tartness of homemade yogurt, I could immediately taste the superior quality of yogurt made with raw milk and excellent-quality yogurt starter. Learning from a purist allowed me to really experience the difference between "real" and "artificial." I feel so happy to start my day with a bowl of homemade yogurt, drizzled with a little pure maple syrup and a handful of walnuts.

For the kids, I add a tablespoon of jam or sweetened fruit.

Peach Pie with Maya

On a balmy August day in New England, my ten-year-old daughter, Maya, and I hopped on our bikes and headed out to see what we could see. We noted her new school, the height of the corn, the kids in the neighborhood. We were giddy with freedom after a family vacation that had us confined inside an RV for two weeks. Instead of our rigid national park planned itinerary, we could go wherever our bikes took us. After thirty minutes of carefree pedaling in the extreme ninety-degree heat, Maya and I were so famished that we made a beeline to Verrill Farms, our local family-owned farm stand extraordinaire.

Upon arriving, we were instantly entranced by a gorgeous basket of local ripe peaches. The entire area was saturated with the smell of sweet, warm juice of fleshy pink fruit. Our sneakers stuck to the floor where the juice had dripped from the peaches. Maya began loading a green basket with choice peaches, fingers sticky with the task. Before I knew it, we were planning whether or not we should make our peach pie with a lattice or crumb topping. The peaches, just a bit past ripe, oozing juice, were selected as pie candidates. In no time, we had a full basket.

We each selected one peach for a snack and sat down next to our bikes and devoured them. Juices streaming down our mouths and dripping on to our shirts, we did not care how we appeared to the other shoppers. Finally, having tied our plastic bag of peaches to the handlebar at such an angle as to not collide with my pedaling knee, we triumphantly delivered the peaches to our kitchen only slightly bruised by the ride.

Looking around the kitchen at our workspace for pie making, I sighed. Suitcases packed with dirty laundry and kitchen camping equipment cluttered the counters. I took a deep breath and decided that all this could wait, dragging everything not conducive to pie baking to the corner of the room. I cleared our work surface and began to focus only on the moment. To hell with order. We were about to embark on pie creation.

Meanwhile, Maya saw none of these things as obstacles; she simply pulled out the cherry wood stool and began looking for the pie plates buried deeply in a high cabinet. I started reading off titles for peach pie recipes. "Car-a-mal, that's the one I want to make," Maya squealed. Feigning deafness, I read several other recipes that seemed simpler, trying to tempt her away from this complex recipe that might overwhelm her halfway through the task, but she insisted. "Are you sure, Maya? This one is quite complicated. We might be here for hours." She nodded her head up and down, stating, "I've always wanted to make a peach caramel pie with lattice top." Knowing that she had never ever heard about it before, I just smiled in agreement. And so, we began our task, donning our aprons over our shorts and pitter-pattering around the cool tile floor in bare feet. The next three hours found us peeling, collecting juice, rolling out crusts, caramelizing sugar and weaving a lattice. Maya chattered happily away, flour dusting her nose, and the kitchen buzzed with our energy. Once she looked over at me in amazement while we sat peeling peaches and said, "How do you peel those so fast? Look, you've done more than half the pile and I've only finished one!" I smiled and answered, "I've been doing this for thirty-six years—you'll be faster than me in no time." As I said this, I felt the significance of that moment, her realizing that she would grow in her pie-making competency.

The recipe Maya selected would have challenged the most proficient of pastry chefs, yet she persevered. The hours we spent together, heads bent to our task, transforming a basket of peaches into a magnificent piece of art emitting an aroma fit to lure the Pied Piper and all the children of Concord, MA where we were living,were treasured moments. Similar moments I had spent with my mother and she with hers. The tradition may have lost its practical roots with few people willing to make their own pie crust, but the source of grounding, the sharing of secrets for how to approach a difficult crust and how to taste sugar levels instead of blindly following the recipe, are sources of knowing, of trusting your own sense of taste, feel and season. We weren't seduced by marketing but by our awareness that those peaches in the basket were a gift waiting to be honored.

The following week, school would begin, our days would become over-scheduled, and I knew we would lose the ability to respond to a peach in this way. We would calculate how many hours it takes to bake a pie and just go out and buy one. But this day, Maya smiled as she looked at me and asked, "How about blueberry crumb tomorrow?" I laughed, surprised by her response. I knew then that she was a pie maker, and the tradition would live on.

Lattice Peach Pie

Ingredients:

Serves 8

Crust:
- 2 pie crusts (I use a regular pate brisée recipe, though frozen is OK, or your favorite pie crust recipe)
- 1 egg white, beaten til frothy

Filling:
- 1 cup sugar, divided
- ½ teaspoon (scant) ground cinnamon
- pinch of salt
- 3 ½ pounds firm but ripe peaches, peeled, halved, pitted, each half cut into 3 wedges
- 1 tablespoon fresh lemon juice
- 1 teaspoon lemon grated lemon rind
- ¼ cup water
- 2 tablespoons (¼ stick) unsalted butter
- 2 tablespoons whipping cream
- 3 tablespoons all-purpose flour
- 1 egg yolk, beaten to blend with 2 teaspoons water (glaze)
- 1 tablespoon sugar mixed with ¼ teaspoon ground cinnamon (cinnamon sugar)

Directions:

To make the crust:
1. Position rack in center of oven and preheat to 375°.
2. Roll out 1 pie crust on lightly floured surface. Transfer to 9-inch-diameter glass pie pan. Trim overhang to 1 inch. Fold edges under and crimp

decoratively, forming high rim (about ½ inch above sides of dish). Chill crust 30 minutes.

3. Line crust with foil; fill with dried beans. Bake crust until sides are set and pale golden, about 35 minutes. Transfer to rack; remove foil and beans. Brush warm crust with egg white. Cool completely.
4. Meanwhile, line another baking sheet with parchment paper. Roll out second pie crust disk on floured surface to 13 ½ -inch round. Cut into ¾-inch-wide strips. Place strips on prepared baking sheet. Chill while preparing filling.

To make the filling:
1. Combine ½ cup sugar, cinnamon, and salt in large bowl.
2. Add peaches, lemon juice and rind and toss gently to coat. Let stand 30 minutes.
3. Meanwhile, stir remaining ½ cup sugar and ¼ cup water in medium saucepan over medium heat until sugar dissolves. Increase heat; boil without stirring until syrup is deep amber, occasionally swirling pan and brushing down sides with wet pastry brush, about 11 minutes. Remove from heat.
4. Add butter and cream (mixture will bubble vigorously); stir caramel until smooth.
5. Strain juices from peaches into caramel; cool to lukewarm.
6. Preheat oven to 375°. Add caramel and flour to peaches in bowl; toss gently. Transfer filling to crust.
7. Arrange 6 dough strips in 1 direction across top of pie, spacing apart. Working with 1 strip at a time, arrange 6 strips in opposite direction atop first, lifting strips and weaving over and under, forming lattice. Gently press ends of strips to edge of baked bottom crust to adhere. Trim overhang. Brush lattice strips (but not crust edge) with egg yolk glaze. Sprinkle strips with cinnamon sugar.
8. Bake pie 35 minutes. Tent pie loosely with foil to prevent over-browning. Continue to bake until filling bubbles and crust is golden brown, ~25 minutes more. Cool completely.

Chinese Chicken Salad

Every time I think about Chinese Chicken Salad, I'm brought back to the weeks following my son Nicolai's birth in July 1994 in Santa Clara, California. If I told you that each tangy, salty mouthful was accompanied by a pang of grief, you might wonder who in their right mind would continue making this dish. Yet this salad wasn't the source of grief; it was the sustenance that got me through a hard time. As I mix the dressing of sesame oil, soy sauce, rice wine vinegar and sugar, my eyes fill with tears. I think of the women who supported my family during those postpartum days, especially Julie Gutierrez-Muegge. She wrote the recipe down for me on a Garfield Post-it while I sat at her kitchen table. She then shared with me what her Mexican grandmother said about childbirth. "Every woman visits the valley of death when giving birth, and some are lucky enough to return to tell about it." Julie reminded me that I was one of the lucky ones. Chinese Chicken Salad helped me to believe that.

Fifteen years later, my son, Nicolai, just home from soccer, put in his order for Chinese Chicken Salad. "Mom, tomorrow will you make Chinese Chicken Salad? I've been telling the guys about it and they're coming over tomorrow night just to eat it. I dream about that salad!" I agree. He can't possibly know what this request means for me. Yes, it is wonderful that he's not asking for pizza or pasta for the thousandth time. But what I am referring to is the nostalgic significance this recipe has for me—and indirectly him.

On January 1, 1994, my husband Carl, my 18-month-old son, Kyle, and I (barely showing my early pregnancy) boarded an airplane in Indianapolis and flew west to Santa Clara. We were starting a new life on the West Coast, near high-tech Silicon Valley and warm weather. My job for the next six months was to entertain an active toddler while incubating a baby. I loved the prospects of exploring a new place and immediately joined Las Madres, a unique mother and child support group. Every week, I would race to the back page of the paper to check the playground location and times and plan everything else around the Las Madres gathering. Before I knew it, Kyle and I had an instant community. What a way to become familiar with the area! We met in a different park every week, so I grew to know of a wide range of play options as well as learning which pediatricians were taking new patients, what days the farmers' markets came to town, and the real pay dirt of the group: names and numbers of good babysitters.

What I didn't anticipate was the support this group would become after the birth of my son. Nico was born without his right leg and hip. It was a huge surprise since the ultrasound didn't pick up the abnormality. The weeks after his birth were filled with the aftermath of shock, medical visits, and the demands of my other son. Every night another meal would arrive from a Las Madres family. The generosity was touching, and after two months we were astounded as the meals just kept coming. Lasagna and casseroles were tough to eat since none of us was very hungry, and the July heat was oppressive in our third-floor condo. So, each time a Chinese Chicken Salad arrived, I ate it. It was the only dish that really appealed to me.

Having a cool salad that felt so nourishing and spring-like brought me hope. I don't know if the dish was in vogue or if it was a regional dish, but we just couldn't seem to get enough of it, and every week several arrived. Cilantro, toasted almonds, sesame seed oil, crunchy romaine, roasted chicken with the skin on; the recipe ingredients varied little and were a symphony of flavors.

Chinese Chicken Salad

Ingredients:

Serves 6

Salad
- 1 head of Romaine lettuce, torn in bite-sized pieces
- ½ bunch chopped fresh cilantro
- 4 green onions, thinly sliced at an angle using ½ of green and white stalk
- ½ cup toasted sliced almonds
- 1 whole rotisserie-roasted chicken, sliced in small pieces
- 15 won ton wrappers, sliced in strips, and fried or 1 can prepared Chow Mein Noodles

Dressing
- 1 teaspoon salt
- ½ teaspoon pepper
- 4 tablespoons Japanese rice wine vinegar
- 2 tablespoons sugar
- ¼ cup canola oil
- 1 tablespoon toasted sesame oil

Directions:

To Make the Salad
1. Layer in the order of the above ingredients list.
2. Pour dressing over the top, toss and serve.

To Make the Dressing
1. Whisk together until sugar is dissolved.

Frying wonton strips adds an additional 15 minutes to the total cooking time.

The Girl Scouts & The Rainbow Salad

I became really embarrassed by my mother when I went to junior high school. I wanted to melt into the background when she wore her powder blue chiffon headscarf tied under her chin. I hated her habit of stuffing tissues up the cuff of her sleeve, often to fall out when she walked down the aisle at church. I was mortified to have friends see her saving cellophane to later wrap leftovers in or the plastic bags washed and hanging to dry from the hood of the stove with magnets.

Not surprisingly, my practical and resourceful mother was also my Girl Scout leader. Imagine my feelings as she stood in front of all the girls in my troop, wearing her brown suede cowboy jacket with the fringe dangling from her sleeve, shaking the jar to make home-made butter, while absolutely no one was paying attention. After the meeting, girls told me that my mom was mean, when really she'd just lost her temper with their bad behavior—or, given her age, maybe a hot flash?

It was funny how, thirty years later, standing in my dining room in front of my daughter's fourth-grade Girl Scout troop, I was so much more sympathetic. Wearing jeans, sneakers and a utilitarian dark colored t-shirt, I was poised to give what I hoped would be a fun cooking lesson that my daughter would be proud to have her mother conduct. Ringing a meditation chime, I gained the girls' attention with only minimal eye-rolling.

I began the activity by asking the girls to read off the foods from their twenty-four-hour food journal—homework assigned at the last meeting. Another mother, acting as scribe, wrote down the names of the food cited: Lucky Charms, bagels with cream cheese, chicken nuggets, peanut butter and jelly sandwiches, milk, Gatorade, tater tots, applesauce and mac and cheese. We stopped then and pulled out our huge rainbow drawing and taped it to the wall. I asked the girls to look at the list and draw a line from the food to the corresponding color on the rainbow. Besides a line from Gatorade to the blue arc, there were no other lines drawn. The girls had a dull color palate of food: tans and browns. I clapped my hands together and announced that this day we would learn to "eat the rainbow." I was careful not to use any nutritional health terms or label foods with "bad or good," "junk or healthy." I outlined what we would be doing for the rest of the meeting. I felt emboldened by how well things were going and pressed on.

First off, we had to build a food lexicon to work from. I put up a list of words that were prohibited: gross, good, yucky, yummy, nasty, bad. Then I pulled out a Tupperware tray with twenty different compartments packed with a mystery food. These would be the components for our food word game. I asked girls to tell me words that were used to describe foods. Collaboratively they called out, "Tart!" "Bitter!" "Sweet!" "Sour!" "Pungent!" "Spicy!" "Savory!" then "Yucky." "Hey," another girl said, "that's against the rules!" The first girl nodded sheepishly. Satisfied with how fast they caught on, I smiled and proceeded. Each girl got to take a turn choosing a food to taste—then picked a matching adjective to describe the taste sensation. When they got to fish sauce and dried mushrooms, "pungent" became a well-used word as they cautiously avoided "gross and yucky." This gave us an excellent opportunity to talk about how some foods are used in conjunction with others that complement them and are never eaten alone.

Now charged up to embrace colorful foods and armed with a wide array of adjectives, we headed to the kitchen. Girls divided themselves among the three stations. "Wow, real knives," one girl exclaimed while another, trying on her paper chef hat, was figuring out what to do about her ponytail. The helping mothers at each site guarded the equipment by standing in front of their stations with arms folded, looking concerned. I hurried through a quick talk about hygiene and safety. Maya demonstrated her version of the knife Circle of Safety by wielding a white plastic knife and twirling around in place. "Good enough," I thought as the last girl rubbed hand sanitizer up to her elbows, laughing obnoxiously to get attention.

The menu was pretty simple: omelets, fruit salad and rainbow salad. In the center of the counter was a mountain of fresh produce, herbs and spices. Eggs and cheese were really the only animal products—not that I ever said a word promoting vegetarianism. I was on a roll to let this experiential learning unfold naturally. As the girls chopped and chatted, the buzz around the room became joyous—women's and girls' voices happily co-mingled with stories and laughter. The colors were magnificent, and when one harried mother declared as she raced into my house to retrieve her daughter before going on to the next carpool stop, "Hey, this is the best meal we've had all week," there was a silent knowing on the faces of all of the moms that spoke volumes: "Yeah, this is so sad but so true."

"Mrs. Calabria, is there any fruit left?" I looked over and noticed that all the omelets and fruit were gone but the Rainbow Salad in the middle of the counter remained practically untouched. I panicked, thinking this was the whole point of the lesson and they weren't even trying it. Refusing to admit defeat, I said in an authoritative voice, "Girls, don't forget about the Rainbow Salad," as I picked it up and placed it in the middle of the table where most of the girls had congregated. The girls all went silent except for one who looked at me shyly, clearly making an effort to choose her words carefully, "I don't think anybody likes beets, Mrs. Calabria." "Oh, but…OK," I said as I swallowed back my disappointment. I had to brace myself not to break my own rule and say how healthy beets were. I picked up the dish again and placed it on the counter near the moms. They devoured it and I had a restored hope that maybe this salad was an acquired taste.

When the Girl Scouts cleaned the kitchen "better than how you found it," my own mother's sage Girl Scout wisdom having come in handy at the end of the messy activity and a mountain of dirty dishes, I smiled at my sparkly, clean counters with only fingerprints on the fridge to remind me that minutes ago there had been 10 rambunctious girls cooking there. I high-fived my mom's spirit, which I felt had been presiding over the meeting. Then I looked over to see Maya helping herself to a big bowl of cereal and milk. "What are you doing?" I asked. "I'm hungry," she said without any remorse. "Nobody likes all that healthy food, Mom, the girls just ate it so you wouldn't get mad. You are kinda weird about food." Ugh, I thought, maybe it's progress that I didn't lose my temper like my mother did.

Well, at least I hadn't taken the easy route and provided sickeningly sweet frostings and artificially colored sprinkles to make high marks with the kids. Instead, I took the Girl Scout motto to heart and modeled courage, confidence and, if I can indulge myself, made the world a better place through exposing girls to whole foods and the joy of cooking.

Chopped Rainbow Salad

Ingredients:

Serves 8
- 2 heads lettuce, shredded
- 2 large carrots, cut into matchstick-size pieces
- 1 yellow and 1 red pepper, cut into matchstick-size pieces
- 3 beets, cooked peeled, and cut into match-size pieces
- 1 cucumber, peeled, seeded, and coarsely chopped
- 4 Japanese radishes, sliced paper thin
- 1 small head of kohlrabi, shredded
- 1 head radicchio, shredded
- chopped flat-leaf parsley, for garnish
- micro-greens for garnish
- gomasio*

Directions:

1. Scatter shredded lettuce on a serving platter. Arrange vegetables in separate rows on top of lettuce.
2. Drizzle Sesame Dressing over salad (see following recipe), sprinkle with parsley and micro greens, add more pepper and sprinkle with gomasio and serve.

Sesame Dressing

Ingredients:
- 3 tablespoons white sesame seeds
- ⅔ cup canola oil (or combination of sesame oil and sunflower oil)
- 3 tablespoons lemon juice
- 2 tablespoons Braggs Liquid Aminos (or tamari)
- 2 tablespoons tahini
- 2 tablespoons chopped fresh chives
- 2 tablespoons chopped parsley
- 2 teaspoons ground mustard
- ½ teaspoon salt (preferably sea salt)
- ⅛ teaspoon cayenne
- ⅛ teaspoon black pepper
- ½ cup water

Directions:
1. Dry roast seeds for 5 minutes or until toasted.
2. Combine all ingredients in a blender or food processor.
3. Serve or refrigerate.

Mom's Secret Brownies

What could possess a former pastry chef to substitute tofu and applesauce in her coveted brownie recipe for butter and eggs? Fat. Not around my belly, but in my brain. I was training for a career in nutrition and the recent book I had read left me convinced that brain health is directly related to the percentage and types of fats we consume. It scared me into trying a new brownie recipe. I compared our family's diet to the one that Michael A. Schmidt writes about in Smart Fats and the tally didn't look good.

So, I stealthily started "Mission Good Fats." Tofu became the likely candidate to replace the half a pound of butter and three eggs in my brownie recipe. You might ask, why not just stop baking brownies? I wasn't ready to give up on the homey smell of chocolate baking. Come on, who can raise a household of teens without the occasional brownie? If I could slip the healthy ingredients into our favorite recipe without them knowing, then why not do it? Try getting those same boys to eat Schmidt's prescribed diet of flax meal, ground chia seeds and wildcaught salmon for their essential oils and you might as well sign them all up for ballroom dance class too.

After I announced that I was going to make brownies, my nine-year-old daughter asked if she could help out. I acted like I hadn't heard her so that I wouldn't have to admit to the ingredient list. That didn't deter her. Knowing that if she stuck around, she'd get to lick the bowl kept her my constant companion. I felt the first beads of sweat form as I performed the first step, cooking tofu, flour and water in a small saucepan. This concoction resembled the beginnings of nursery school playdough. Luckily, Maya liked to make playdough and noted nothing out of the ordinary as she stirred the glutinous slop. I sighed and bent to my next step, careful not to utter my own misgivings. By the time the melted chocolate had been stirred into the tofu mixture along with the vanilla and nuts, no one would have guessed that this was anything but brownie batter. I scraped the contents into my prepared pan and popped it into the oven. Maya sat happily on the counter licking the bowl with her finger, never questioning the missing butter and eggs. Now I just had to wait to see if I had accomplished my mission.

After twenty minutes of baking, the familiar chocolaty aroma started wafting through the house and I heard video-hazed teen voices call from the basement inquiring if there were any brownies for them. I smiled smugly. I may just have fooled them all! If I admitted that there was tofu in the brownies, no one would even eat the smallest tidbit. They wouldn't care how many expensive organic ingredients I used. Tofu might as well be stamped "biohazard" in this household.

I cleaned the kitchen, thoroughly burying any evidence of my healthy campaign deep at the bottom of the garbage can, and then I called sweetly, "Brownies are ready." Stampeding up the stairs, each boy grabbed a warm brownie and devoured it with no questions asked. Their faces were blissful as they consumed brownie after brownie before going back to the basement for the next round of video games.

A few minutes later, my tofu-hating husband sauntered in and cut himself a piece. He chewed thoughtfully and then put it down, asking, "Is something different with the brownies?" I smiled triumphantly and said, "Tofu." He replied, "I thought so, the only food on the planet that actually takes away taste, leaving you with a net negative mouthful," and he turned leaving the uneaten half sitting on the counter. I shrugged and picked up the remainder and ate it, thinking, well four out of five thumbs up is still a net positive.

Mom's Secret Brownies

Ingredients:
Makes 16 Brownies
- ⅓ cup cocoa powder
- 1 scant cup semisweet chocolate, chopped (about 4 ounces)
- 4 ounces unsweetened chocolate (usually packaged as one-ounce bars)
- 1¼ cups granulated sugar
- 1 cup silken tofu, blended in a blender or food processor
- ½ cup sunflower or canola oil
- 2 teaspoons vanilla extract
- ¾ cup spelt flour
- ½ teaspoon baking powder
- ½ teaspoon coarse salt
- 1 cup semisweet chocolate chips (optional)
- ½ cup walnuts, chopped (optional)

Directions:
1. Preheat oven to 350°. Line an 8-inch square baking pan with parchment paper and dust with cocoa powder.
2. In a double boiler, melt semisweet and unsweetened chocolate together. Stir continually with a heat-proof spatula to prevent burning or hardening, about 5 minutes.
3. Mix in the cocoa powder and remove the pan from the heat.
4. In a large bowl, combine sugar, tofu, oil and vanilla with a rubber spatula.
5. Stir in melted chocolate, then the flour, baking powder, salt and optional chocolate chips and walnuts.
6. Pour batter into baking pan, making sure that it spreads evenly. Bake for 35 to 40 minutes, until slightly puffed and toothpick inserted comes out clean.
7. Remove from oven and let cool in the pan for two hours before cutting into squares. Dust with powdered sugar.

I dust with powdered sugar over a paper doily for special occasions.

Annette's Brownies

Ingredients:

Makes 20 Brownies
- 2 sticks unsalted butter
- 4 ounces unsweetened chocolate, broken into small pieces
- 4 eggs
- 2 cups sugar
- 1 teaspoon vanilla extract
- 1 ½ (scant) cups all-purpose flour
- 8 ounces mini-chocolate chips (optional)
- powdered sugar for dusting

Directions:

1. Preheat oven to 350°.
2. Melt butter with unsweetened chocolate in a medium-sized saucepan on low heat, stirring constantly.
3. Beat eggs and sugar in a medium-sized mixing bowl.
4. Add slightly cooled chocolate mixture and vanilla extract to eggs and sugar.
5. Slowly add flour.
6. Pour into a 9-by-13-inch pan sprayed with canola oil.
7. Sprinkle evenly mini chocolate chips over the top.
8. Bake for 25 minutes. Cool completely before sprinkling with powdered sugar and cutting.

The Mother of a Wrestler

When my son returned from wrestling practice, I was on high alert for opportunities to feed him. Welcome to the life of the mother of a high school wrestler, a wrestler who was intent on preserving his spot on the varsity team by wrestling at the only weight class open, the lightest one, 106 pounds. He was five-feet ten inches tall. I had fully loaded the fridge with all his favorite foods. Only wrestling could possibly have turned my thinking and my kitchen upside down. I used to only stock my cabinets with organic, high nutritive foods, but then I was willing to purchase anything that might have tempted him to eat—even sugar-sweetened cereals.

I watched my seventeen-year-old son, wearing nothing but a maroon singlet, drenched in sweat, eating a single tablespoon of peanut butter from the Skippy jar, sucking on the spoon to extract every last bit. He was hollowed-eyed, and each rib poked through his skin. I resisted the temptation to ask him why he was not eating the organic peanut butter with added flax seeds that we usually consumed. I knew his response already.

When he reached for a protein drink in a can, I broke my silence with an offer to make him a smoothie. Relief—he acquiesced, and I raced to the blender, grabbing up all the nutritional additives I could possibly find that wouldn't sabotage the flavor. It would be a challenge for any mother and for me; it was where I most wanted to succeed in my quest for nutritional expertise. I proffered up a glass of frothy pink goodness and completed it with a large-diameter plastic straw that my sister gave me to make my own bubble tea at home. This added feature made my smoothies more appealing to my kids, I think. I watched as he took his first drag on the straw. His face registered nothing. He turned and went upstairs with his drink. I was frozen in place then nodded in acceptance of his nonplussed response. This round was a success.

Later that week, I taught an Intentional Eating class. I asked women to tell their "food stories" and I realized that I need to come clean with a new chapter in mine—the one about being the mother of a 106-pound, five-foot ten-inch wrestler. This was one of those times that I could not speak with any authority. I did not know how to navigate these nutritional waters. I was versed in the opposite dialogue of overeating and self-sabotage with food. For someone who could quote chapter and verse of almost any food fad, calorie content and nutritional trivia, I was embarrassed that I could not even raise with Nico the possibility of what he was doing to his body through this nutritional deprivation. He didn't want to know that this was the last time in his life that he could build bones or that he was killing neurological synapses and that was why he was not able to concentrate in school.

He went to bed at regularly at seven o'clock and couldn't focus on schoolwork; all this with a single-minded determination to weigh 106 pounds by that Saturday morning. By the way, did I mention that by Friday he was six pounds over his goal? If one of my clients told me that they were planning to lose six pounds in a day, I would not hesitate to refer them to a psychiatrist. Because I knew that the only way they could achieve this goal would be by using health-damaging methods like laxatives, vomiting and excessive exercise. I didn't ask him which he would use because I didn't really want to know. Denial is a powerful parenting tool.

Who was to blame for this parenting dilemma? I felt angry with my husband and my son's coach. To be that powerless was every bit as frustrating as dealing with the same boy who, as a toddler, refused to eat his dinner. But really I was just looking for a scapegoat for my own ineffectual nutritional counseling. I could talk until I was blue in the face and stock the pantry with healthy foods, but I could not lead him to eat those foods. As I talked to the women on Thursday night to practice the guideline "eat when you are hungry," I thought of how earlier that day I packed a cooler full of food and headed off to the first day of the State Wrestling Tournament to arrive just after weigh-ins so Nico could eat, not when he was hungry, but when he was literally starving. I watched my twelve-year-old daughter dive right into the same cooler, eating as much as Nico, and wondered how this deprivation food model would influence her.

Nico was an extremely successful athlete. It seemed that this success trounced all nutritional wisdom. At that particular tournament, he won all but one match and arrived on the podium Saturday night in third place. He lost only to one opponent, who weighed 125 pounds. Because his opponent was female, she was allowed to wrestle at two weight classes higher. This, Nico explained, was because they didn't want girls to cut so much weight they don't have enough body fat to menstruate. I wondered if she had survived for weeks on only one tablespoon of peanut butter per meal. Ultimately, I signed the medical release form. I signed it trusting that the healthy weight policy and the coach would guide my son in making the right decision. Instead, I watched tongue-tied by what seemed to be bad decision after bad decision spiral into a situation that I could not condone or undo. If I had to do it again, I would have used the same principles to counsel Nico as I do in my Intentional Eating class:

- Eat when you are hungry.
- Stop when you are full.
- Pay attention to your meal, sitting down with no distractions.
- Eat with gusto and pleasure.

And I would not have signed the medical release form. Not making the varsity team as a junior would have been a real blow to Nico's ego since he had wrestled on varsity the year before. But I will never really know what kind of physical damage that period of extreme nutritional depravation had on Nico's body. The risk that he took was unnecessarily dangerous and the adults in his life really did let him down.

Nico, Maya and Kyle

A Night at the Smoothie Factory

When my kids were younger, Sunday night was Family Night. This meant from five to seven we had time together as a family. This ranged from making pizzas to going to see a movie. But with the lives of teenagers, Family Night has changed, with the last relics looking more like a family dinner with little time invested by anyone but me.

So, out of the drudgery of planning another meal, I came up with "Smoothie Factory." On Friday I went to the market and purchased a large variety of frozen fruits, juices and nuts to make healthy albeit tasty smoothies. My goal was for each individual to come up with their favorite combination of ingredients and record the concoction so they could replicate it. Every morning I make myself a smoothie, and it was time to get the family on board. I often heard how my morning smoothie was disgusting—referred to as "pond scum" by one son. To which I usually responded, "That's how I keep my six pack," jokingly pulled up my shirt to show off my belly. Though I had to admit, he had a point. Kale and blueberries whirled in the blender look pretty unappetizing, but the health benefits still kept me coming back.

As the hour approached, I reminded everyone that we would be having smoothie night at five o'clock. Soon Kyle realized that he had forgotten about a graduation party he had planned to attend, and Nico gave me an ultimatum: "Either I attend family night and fail my biology test, or I skip it and ace my test." Chastising them both for not planning ahead, I resigned myself to making the best of the shrinking group.

As the rain steadily came down and the chilly weather began to dampen my resolve, I wondered if it was more of a soup day. Maybe this was just one of those ideas that I had gotten too attached to. Just as I began to put all the frozen fruit away, my husband walked in and said, "Let's make smoothies. I've been dreaming about these all day!" I kissed him passionately. He's always late to dinner and usually could not care less about food, but when it comes to cold blender drinks, he's a big fan. Maya walked in and goggled at all the ingredients lined up on the counter for her slurping pleasure.

I first went over the rules of the evening: everyone needed to measure their ingredients and record them as they went along. They received extra points for choosing ingredients from each section: frozen fruit, liquids, protein sources, greens, essential oils. I then explained what some of the ingredients were, like chia seeds and hemp milk. I invited them to sample everything before we began, but they were too eager to delay. They wanted to roll up their sleeves and start blending.

Carl volunteered to be first. He announced that his smoothie would be pink. He went right for the frozen fruit. He added mostly berries and then as an afterthought threw in a banana. He then looked at the other groupings of food and added juice for his liquid and then turned on the blender. His smoothie was a beautiful rose color. He stopped the machine and used a teaspoon to dig out a taste. He smacked his lips together and announced that it needed something sour; it was too sweet. So, I peeled an entire lemon and did a little seed mining, then threw it whole into the blender. He whipped it up again and retried his concoction. Smiling broadly, he announced it ready to be served. Maya and I hastily lined up to taste as Carl poured with pride his pink smoothie. It was, I have to admit, quite delicious. I couldn't help but ask, "You know what's mostly in this, don't you?" Maya announced, "Sugar and water, with some vitamins and minerals." "Yes," I replied. Carl looked a little dejected and dumped in a scoop of vanilla protein powder and re-blended. The result was an overpowering vanilla flavor. We all agreed his original smoothie was better and it might be better to just serve this smoothie with scrambled eggs than add the protein powder.

Maya was up next. She went right for the frozen mangoes. Nothing had changed. That same girl at age two would sit on the deck holding an entire mango with both hands, juice dripping down her chin and onto her belly. She added raspberries, flax oil and chia seeds. The color was that of a beautiful sunset: pink, coral and orange. The taste was wonderful, smooth, tropical, and refreshing. Given how gray the past six days had been with constant rain, their colorful blender drinks were lightening everyone's spirits.

Next, I was up. I knew that my smoothie would be green. I feel so good when I eat a lot of greens and really I can eat about three times the quantity of greens in a blender drink than I can in a salad. So in went half a bag of baby spinach, frozen pineapple tidbits, half a cucumber, chia seeds and a half a banana to make it sweet enough. I didn't add any protein powder since the chia seeds had some protein. The color was a pale green, and it was the consistency of a creamsicle. Everyone liked it who was willing to try it.

Kyle walked in just as we were sampling mine, and he rolled his eyes. "I'm not trying the Green Monster," he said. Instead, he went right for Maya's cup and finished it in one swell slurp. I begged him to try mine, enticing him with, "You're going to love it; even your dad thought it was his favorite." So, I lied a little. Beaten down enough, he reticently took a small spoonful. He smacked his lips together and said, "Tastes like cucumbers…yours always taste like cucumbers." "Well, do you like it?" I asked. "Nope. I want a pink smoothie, not green, Mom."

The next week Maya and a friend decided to make smoothies for an after-school snack, claiming we didn't have anything else decent for snacking on in the house. I reminded her of the index card that she had written her smoothie recipe on, now taped on the outside of the fridge. The next thing I knew she had recreated her smoothie, omitting bananas since we were out. I was happy that the Smoothie Factory lived on.

The following week I received a phone call from Kyle asking me if by any chance the smoothie he made could have given him a headache. When I found out that he put in every possible ingredient in the fridge including fish oil, flax oil, hemp milk and protein powder, I felt a little nauseated. I replied, "Maybe you should have come to the Smoothie Factory, my dear!"

Calabria Smoothie Classics

Maya's Mango Blast
Makes 1 serving
- 1 ripe mango
- 1 ripe banana
- 1 scoop vanilla protein powder (Mercola's)
- ⅔ cup crushed ice
- ½ cup orange mango juice
- 1 tablespoon flax seed oil

Carl's Pink Smoothie
1 Makes 1 serving
- 1 cup frozen raspberries
- 1 banana (frozen all the better)
- ½ part orange juice
- 1 lemon peeled and seeded

Jeanine's Green Monster
Makes 1 serving
- ½ cup frozen pineapple tidbits
- ½ sliced cucumber
- 2 handfuls of fresh spinach or other green
- ½ of a frozen banana
- 1 tablespoon of crushed chia seeds (put in blender first before adding other ingredients and crush)
- ½ cup of water

Virgin Rose
Makes 1 serving
- 1 part tart cherry juice (100% juice)
- 3 parts seltzer water
- 3 parts orange juice
- ½ part lemon juice
- splash of grenadine syrup

A Night at the Smoothie Factory - 159

Kyle and his friends pose for a promo photo for my cooking classes

4. Eating Green and Clean

Lime Jello and Swiss Chard on the Same Table

"Trade you my raspberries for your Hostess Ding Dong," I said, reaching into my Partridge Family lunch box and pulling out the baggie full of tart, red berries. Julie Crawford, my fourth-grade best friend who sat next to me most lunch times, grabbed for the baggie. I'd picked the ruby gems the afternoon before and knew that they were as fresh as could be. I then very slowly and ceremoniously began to peel away the thin silver foil covering of the Ding Dong and licked off the outside layer of dipped chocolate that covered the cake with such relish that even now I salivate remembering…

That lunch was what helped me recognize the validity of the nutritional training I received as an adult. I knew then that picked from my back yard was better than foil wrapped processed cakes. Yet it hadn't kept me from wanting to try it all: real, processed, gourmet, junk…part of what I'd learn that day in my first class as "eating from the entire food palette." How else can the jeweler distinguish paste from precious stones but by having them both side by side and witnessing the difference in the way they feel, look and reflect light? The same can be said about food: experiencing fake and real helps build an expertise in discerning the difference.

The nutritional training I received in my forties studying with Hale Sofia Schatz helped me to synthesize a lifetime of eating research. "Source, source, source," cried out the petite sixty-year-old woman whose full head of auburn curls danced as she pointed in the air accentuating each word. I was mesmerized as I watched my beloved teacher make her point. "Never believe the claims on the front of the package. Be sure you know where your food really comes from, track it down, don't just ask the clerk at Whole Foods."

Though I never would have said it like that, I innately understood what she was talking about. Like any good teacher, instead of spoon feeding me facts, Hale required her students to pull forth the knowledge from within and prodded them in just the right ways to have that "aha moment." Her teaching was transformative and always mildly edgy. Though I did not always agree with her training tactics, I respected her food wisdom. She did not advocate fads or trends, but instead pointed to ancient cultural practices surrounding food and health. The healthy emotional and physical impact that transpires when people are directly involved with the growing and preparation of the food that they eat became quite evident. Though I had read about how the "stress hormone" cortisol played a part in keeping people overweight, this had little impact on my own lifestyle changes. But following her experience-based practices did. Besides participating and training to become a cleanse instructor, I began going to local farms, joining CSAs, and starting my own raised veggie beds. My stress level decreased as I became more active with my own food production—I became happier and more present.

I was a student of food. I loved learning about it and knew that I had a gift for cooking and in particular making the most nutritious foods taste good. I'd cooked for restaurants and camps, but was ready to add nutritional training to my resumé. Attending her program soon after losing both my parents was no coincidence. This woman seemed to know things I did not. I wanted to learn how to eat in a way that could inoculate me from getting cancer.

Everything she said seemed completely different from anything else I'd ever heard about food, yet it resonated with what I knew intrinsically from being raised in a family that grew their own fruits and veggies. "When you see the soil, the growing environment and how the produce is handled, there are no mysteries." I learned a lot about CSAs (community supported agriculture) that summer, how in Japan a CSA literally translates to "see the farmer's face." I immediately joined one. Participating in a CSA introduced me to recipes and vegetables that I had never tried, but when confronted with my weekly CSA share of kohlrabi and Japanese radish, I found some real treasures.

I grew up sitting at the kitchen table with Swiss chard just picked from the garden placed side-by-side with the artificially flavored lime Jello and cottage cheese that my mother referred to as salad. What I had been raised eating served as my raw material—a lifetime of food experiments. During the twenty-one days attending her workshop, I learned from Hale how to bring forth what I already really knew. She helped me articulate this understanding and build a discipline around how I would cook and eat going forward.

Lesson #1: Know the face of the farmer who grows your food.

Cheesy Kale Chips

Ingredients:

Makes 4 cups
- 1 bunch of kale or spinach—older, firmer leaves are better (remove tough center stems by ripping out the middle), washed and patted dry
- olive oil
- sea salt

Directions:

1. Line 3 to 4 baking sheets with parchment paper. Preheat oven to 300°.
2. Toss kale/spinach with ¼ cup of Raw Cheesy Dressing.
3. Run each leaf between your fingers to take off excess dressing. The leaf should be lightly coated, not dripping with the dressing.
4. Arrange each leaf on baking sheet so that sides do not touch. Bake for 20 minutes.
5. Remove from oven and turn each leaf over. Return to oven to bake 10 to 20 minutes longer or until leaves are crispy. Cool completely before removing to an air-tight container to store.

Raw Cheesy Dressing

Ingredients:
- 1¼ cup raw cashews, pieces OK (soaked in cold water for 1-2 hours)
- 1 cup of water
- juice of 1 lemon
- 2 pinches sea salt
- 2 pinches garlic powder
- 2 pinches onion powder
- 2 pinches cayenne

Directions:
1. Drain the soaked cashews. Place all ingredients in a blender and blend until completely smooth, stopping to scrape sides down.

(Use for Kale Chips)

Greens with Beans

Ingredients:
Serves 6
- 2 tablespoons olive oil
- 2 leeks, sliced thin
- 6 cloves garlic, chopped small
- 1 pound greens cut into -1-inch strips (beet greens are beautiful mixed with spinach, but any greens work)
- juice of one lemon
- 1 bay leaf
- 14 ounces veggie broth
- 1 28-ounce can of tomatoes, diced and including juice
- 1 15-ounce can cannellini beans, drained
- 1½ teaspoon sea salt
- ¼ teaspoon dried chipotle pepper or if you want to avoid the heat add ½ teaspoon smoked paprika
- chopped fresh parsley, optional

Directions:
1. Heat oil and add leeks, garlic and greens. Cook 5 minutes, just until the greens begin to wilt.
2. Add tomatoes with their juice and all other ingredients except the beans. Cook for 15 minutes.
3. Add the drained beans, lemon juice and if you want a cup of fresh, chopped parsley. Cook for 5 minutes, stirring frequently.

Serve with rice or couscous, which absorbs the lovely broth of the greens to make a wonderful vegetarian meal.

Squeezing Grief In

"I'm agnostic, not atheist," my dad would respond when asked why he didn't attend church with the rest of the family. He said he'd have a better chance of finding God in his garden or greenhouse. So, when he died, my sisters and I agreed: no church service. We would emphasize his love of plants. Dad's illness had been unexpected, necessitating rushed departures, and then, an urgency to return once he had passed. Through emails and calls, we set the celebration date for Bastille Day, a month later. I was pleased I would still be able to make it to a nutritional workshop I had long awaited, and which had required me to orchestrate my kids' camp schedules to coincide with my time away. And, besides, Bastille Day was the perfect day for a man fiercely proud of his French heritage and who flew the blue, blanc and rouge outside his lakeside home in rural Indiana.

My sisters and I arrived a few days ahead of the "grand fete" to plan and prepare. Now that the notices had gone out to friends and family, we were hogtied to the free-form, bohemian service barely even outlined on paper. We decided to rent a tent to place over the end of the driveway in case of rain and to use my parents' lakeside home to host the reception; it fit who my father was as a man, lover of nature and king of his "castle." By day two of scouring sinks and chasing away dust bunnies in my parents' empty home, a funeral parlor looked downright welcoming. Why had we felt it necessary to be so authentic to the man we memorialized when my Dad clearly had stated "funerals were for the living"? The venue and avant-garde service preparations overwhelmed me; stealing away the levity I so desired to get through the day ahead.

While politely disagreeing, and then later downright bickering, then, finally, giving each other the silent treatment, my sisters and I prepared food for the reception, divided and repotted a lifetime of house plants as gifts for our guests, and created an outdoor sound system. And yes…we each still had to write our parts of the eulogy.

Once our guests arrived, we were more or less ready, though exhausted and edgy. I perched just behind the makeshift altar, catching an occasional whiff of lemon blossoms from the potted tree at my side. I sat alert and ready to intervene in case of mishaps with the music, the readings, or the speeches. Miraculously, the program flowed seamlessly, poignant, and reflective of the man who was my father. And I was both mourner and event planner. At the end of the day, my sisters and I embraced, all tension melted away by our successful fait accompli.

As my family drove away from the service, guests still mingling over their French cheeses and wines, and "King of the Road" playing on the speakers, I felt we had honored him well. Something for me, however, had yet to be expressed. But life called, and my mind shifted to catching our flight home.

Kids ferried off to camp, my husband back at work, I breathed a sigh of relief. I immediately set off to join a nutritional workshop I was hellbent on attending. Twenty women gathered together in a beautiful old Victorian home. I had met the facilitator at Kripalu (a yoga and retreat center) and admired her food wisdom; I thought I might even become a nutritional counselor. As the workshop progressed and the facilitator kept going on about "letting go" and "releasing that which no longer serves us," I had misgivings. What did this have to do with healthy eating and a career in nutrition?

Before arriving, we were supposed to have given up dairy, sugar, meat, wheat, alcohol and caffeine. So, when our leader came down fairly hard on a woman who was still eating sweetened yogurt with fruit, it felt more like a boot camp than a nutritional workshop. Given my indulgences at my father's memorial service, I was complicit with the "yogurt eater," just less forthcoming. "You are creating a structure to strengthen your resolve and make the changes you aspire to," the facilitator intoned. We were asked to write down something that "no longer served us," to put in the fire bowl outside. As for me, I was distracted, enumerating in my head all the hoops I'd jumped through to make it to this workshop.

Refocusing, I scribbled "grief" on my bit of paper, then got in line behind our leader. We followed her out to her garden. The courtyard was a floral riot of colors, scents and sound; the air was cool and refreshing. Then, I stopped in shock. Before me stood potted fig and lemon trees—the plants my dad had raised so lovingly in his greenhouse. I burst into tears. I realized that this was where I needed to be but not for the reasons I had thought. To hell with event planning and nutritional training; I was here for something else.

Golden Broth

Ingredients:

Makes 2 quarts broth
- 1 onion, chopped
- 1 clove garlic, chopped
- ½ cup yellow split peas
- 1 carrot, chopped
- 1 potato, chopped
- 2 tablespoons olive oil
- ½ teaspoon turmeric
- a few celery leaves
- 2 quarts hot water
- ½ teaspoon salt

Directions:

1. Sauté first 5 ingredients in olive oil.
2. Add water and salt and simmer for 30 minutes.
3. Stir in turmeric, celery leaves and simmer for 5 more minutes. Strain for a thin stock, puree for a thick one.

Nutritional understanding and a good place to replenish after shedding many tears. This broth can be used in lieu of chicken broth.

Christmas popovers, a family tradition

5. Food for Good Times & Bad Times

Life Lessons from My Freezer

One cold January morning, I opened my freezer door to pull out some frozen fruit for a smoothie and a turkey carcass came careening down, landing on my slippered foot. As I rubbed my throbbing big toe, I said "Today is the day I must clean out my freezer." Then I plopped the frozen Thanksgiving souvenir into a large soup pot and proceeded to remove the entire contents of my freezer to take inventory. After close review, I found more than just frozen foods.

Lesson 1 – Don't waste anything

Though I grew up during the 60's, when economic times were good, my mother was a product of the Great Depression and she continued to save everything, a habit she never lost. She even kept the packaging from household items like Charmin toilet paper in lieu of purchasing plastic wrap. As I looked over the contents on my counter, I noticed that I had used many plastic bags multiple times, including a zip-locked chopped pecan bag from Trader Joe's now storing frozen fish. My mother taught me the steps to implementing a waste-free household, but what motivates me to do so differs from what motivated her. The environmental movement has awakened in all of us the understanding that what we are throwing away directly impacts the health of all living beings. Having lost loved ones to cancer and having a child born with a birth defect, I have been very motivated to create a healthy lifestyle and not contribute additionally to the degradation of our planet. My mother's motivation was in direct response to the global economic crisis of the times. As I perused the diversity of foods I've saved on the counter - 1/4 cup chopped onions, combined Tupperware of canned green chiles and chipotle peppers in Adobo sauce, one frozen skinless, boneless chicken breast with a bit of freezer burn - I realized that my mother has given me the ability to see past minor defects and embrace the value of what remains.

Lesson 2 – Limited resources = increased creativity

I started multiple pots of water boiling – the turkey carcass for bone broth and another for chicken tortilla soup to use up the aforementioned ingredients. Solving this food puzzle was at once both exhilarating and practical. Not only would my freezer be clean, but I'd have a couple nights of prepared meals. I love having a limited list of ingredients and finding a way to combine all into a delicious meal. Though I could go out and purchase just about anything I would need to make a specific recipe, the "scarcity," albeit self-imposed, drives my creativity. Having had a lifetime of cooking experiences affording me a diverse palate of culturally rich combinations to draw upon, I am triggered easily into understanding what combinations go together and which ones to avoid. This is where cooking leaves the realm of a ho-hum household task to become a creative art form.

Lesson 3 – Be adventurous and bold or be bored and safe

I follow a recipe when I am tired and need to just get dinner on the table. At low-energy times, it gives me inspiration and the confidence that the ingredients we have on hand will be used in a way that most people find satisfactory. Someone else figures out the ratios and creates the shopping list – but it also gives away the opportunity to create something new, go where no other cook has ventured. So when I take the scarcity cooking risk, I know that I may be in for a flop, but she who never risks... Besides, I can feel some justification that most people would have thrown these ingredients away earlier – so why not use them as the artistic raw materials that might just turn out to be a culinary masterpiece.

Lesson 4 – Abundance, passing it on

When I saw the frozen peaches that I picked last summer, I had to mentally wrestle with myself about making quick breads – having only yesterday vowed no more sweets in the house after the holidays. But it felt like such a waste to whirl them into my daily breakfast smoothie after having lovingly picked each one. So, I threw caution to the wind and began mixing up the batter for a tropical fruit bread, thinking so many people I knew could use a bit of sunshine in the dead of winter. As I pulled out the mini-loaf pans, I created a recipient list of all the people for whom I'm grateful. The list multiplied past the amount of batter I had. This had me considering making granola too with all those frozen pecans and the jumbo package of Costco Craisins. The contents of my freezer began magically supplying enough food to send all my gifts of gratitude.

As I returned to work after my busy freezer-cleaning weekend, I thought about how these lessons were basically the foundation for my work as the leader of a food relief organization. My mother was the lead professor at the school of practical learning, and I was her willing student. Had she accompanied me into the commercial kitchen that day, she would have smiled when she saw the huge ham bone rescued from a local company holiday party now sticking out from the top of the bubbling pot of pea soup. A volunteer was organizing to-go containers destined to supply soup to over 100 families. I would have turned to her and said, "What a legacy you've left, mom," and then invited her in to opine on how to use up the 50 pounds of water chestnuts we had just received.

Tropical Summer Bread

in the Dead of Winter

Ingredients:

Makes 1 loaf
- 1 pound frozen chopped peaches, slightly thawed
- 1 box Trader Joe's banana bread mix
- 1 cup toasted coconut

Directions:
1. Mix all ingredients together with an electric mixer.
2. Pour into a greased and floured loaf pan.
3. Following the baking instructions on the back of the bread mix, bake accordingly.

Channel your inner culinary artist when looking into your freezer - inspiration comes in many forms.

Chicken Tortilla Freezer Soup

Ingredients:

Serves 6
- 1 frozen organic chicken breast, thawed and cut into ½ inch chunks
- 1 quart (approximately) frozen chicken stock
- 1 chopped onion (mine was previously frozen)
- 1 teaspoon (or more depending on your spice tolerance) canned and chopped chipotle peppers in adobe sauce
- ½ can chopped green chilies
- 1 teaspoon cumin
- ½ teaspoon smoked paprika (smoked chipotle is an option for those who like the heat)
- 1 15½-ounce can hominy
- ½ bag frozen corn (approximately 8 ounces)

Directions:

1. Place all ingredients except the hominy, corn and fresh red pepper in a crock-pot.
2. Cook on high or low setting in crock-pot depending on how much time you have before dinner.
3. During the last ½ hour of cooking, add frozen corn, can of hominy and chopped fresh red bell pepper.

Serve with grated cheese, corn tortilla chips, fresh lime juice and plenty of chopped red onion and cilantro.

Lauren and I at St. Peters and Pauls cathedral Kitchen (Indianapolis), feeding those in need since 1981

Me! Happiest cooking for a crowd.

Big Kitchen Cooking

For almost twenty-five years, my sister Lauren has been cooking one Sunday a month for a soup kitchen, specifically the Sunday Cathedral Soup Kitchen at 14th and Pennsylvania in inner-city Indianapolis. On Mother's Day one year, she asked our mother and me to help out. We both accepted and arrived wearing our aprons and baseball caps over our go-out-to-brunch clothes. Both of us were curious and had heard stories about the soup kitchen for years from Lauren. What better way to start off the day than with two generations of women, shoulder to shoulder, in the kitchen?

The men of our family were back at home preparing a Mother's Day dinner. For the next two hours, we helped Lauren haul from her van day-old bakery items and served them with coffee to the mostly male guests who were already lined up outside the dining room despite it being several hours from serving time. The kitchen spirit was light and joyful; we joked and reminisced as we worked together. Soon, however, Lauren discovered that there wasn't any all-purpose flour to thicken the sausage gravy she was planning for the breakfast casserole. For most cooks this would have been a mini-disaster in the making, but not for Lauren. She simply figured out how to thicken sausage gravy with what was on hand; why not Bisquick? Immediately, she'd calculated the need to reduce salt and how to counter the effect of the baking powder; amazingly, she pulled it off.

At the helm of the old gas stove, she spent much of her time with a colorful assortment of spices, tasting spoons and a whisk. She knew what texture and taste she was after as she played around with getting the right mix of flavors in the dish she was creating. The crowd of hungry men loved the food and consumed every last crumb.

Lauren's culinary confidence is legendary. She never seems concerned that there won't be enough or the right ingredients to pull off the meal. When she cooks, her spirit gets channeled right into the dishes she serves.

Ten years later, I was cooking in a soup kitchen. The place was different, though. I was cooking at the Open Table of Maynard in Eastern Massachusetts. Every second Monday of the month, I donned my forest green apron and baseball hat and loaded my car with enough groceries for a meal for one hundred. I missed more than anything now cooking with my family. I had taken for granted those times when we all put on a holiday meal together and now, doing it solo, I was intensely aware of my sister's and mother's absence. You could say I was channeling Lauren and Mom each time I went to cook for Open Table. Phoning Lauren those days often included requests for cooking inspiration. Our calls no longer centered on care for our aging parents; we instead had the pleasure of sharing our mutual passion for food.

Lauren came to the Maynard community kitchen as a guest cook while visiting for my son's graduation. On that particular Monday, the Department of Health came for a surprise inspection. As I answered the firing squad style questioning of the inspector, I saw Lauren quietly standing behind her, nodding reassuringly as I BSed my way through. Big sister comes through once again - I couldn't have been more thankful as my legs and hands were shaking under my apron.

Lauren noticed during her visit that we cooked for a different clientele. She cooked predominately for homeless men who generally preferred spicy food. Our kitchen provided for many elderly who are on fixed incomes and who preferred bland and easy-to-chew food. With Lauren's recipes, I had to hold the pepper and spices and decrease the fat content. Sadly, the plentiful food donations from large box stores had become scarce due to legal counsel advising corporations to protect themselves against potential food contamination suits. At Open Table in Maynard, we were able to cut our cost per dinner in half by using the Greater Boston Food Bank weekly donations.

The challenge for most cooks in soup kitchens is to create a meal that is healthy with limited resources and one that will also appeal to the palates of the clientele. How often did I leave my own health views at the door when I put on my apron and worked with the big pots? The inner narrative was very active. I relied heavily on parsley, cilantro and green onions. I found no one objected to finely minced herbs in everything. I also had come to embrace frozen produce, which was extremely affordable and provided the volume of veggies that I couldn't get with fresh. I also deftly ignored the fifty pounds of meat per meal guideline. The community dinner board firmly maintained that each meal should provide plenty of access to animal protein, since it was otherwise too expensive for many guests to access. Although this was true, I had to disagree that this was preferable if the meat came from US commodities with high levels of fat that cooked down to something resembling gray paste. Instead, I stretched this meat with a mirepoix of celery, onions, carrots, red onions and various herbs, including a paste of chilies, bread, eggs and whole grain breadcrumbs.

"Following are two recipes: a favorite from Lauren's soup kitchen and one from mine."

Lauren's Sausage Gravy

Ingredients:

Serves 100
(8 servings in parentheses)
- 13 pounds good quality lean pork sausage (1 pound)
- 2 pounds butter (¼ cup)
- 3 cups, plus 2 tablespoons all-purpose flour (4 tablespoons)
- 2 gallons whole milk (approximately to desired thickness) (2⅓ cup)
- ⅓ cup onion powder (1 ½ tablespoons)
- 1 tablespoon ground crushed red pepper (dash)
- 3 tablespoons dried sage (½ teaspoon)
- salt and pepper to taste

Directions:

1. Brown the sausage, breaking it into crumbled pieces.
2. Melt the butter into the browned sausage, then add the flour and cook (stirring) for 2 to 3 minutes.
3. Slowly add milk, stirring constantly, until bubbling and thick. Add seasoning to taste.

Serve gravy over fresh biscuits

Lauren's Biscuits

Ingredients:

Makes 100 biscuits
(24 in parentheses)
- 4 ¼ packages active dry yeast (1 package)
- 1 cup and 1 tablespoon warm water (½ cup)
- 8⅓ cups buttermilk (2 cups)
- 21 cups all-purpose flour (5 cups)
- ¼ cup and 1 teaspoon baking powder (1 teaspoon)
- 1 tablespoon and 1 ¼ teaspoons baking soda (1 teaspoon)
- 2 tablespoons and 2 ¼ teaspoons salt (1 teaspoon)
- ¾ cup and 1 teaspoon granulated sugar (¼ cup)
- 3 cups and 2 tablespoons shortening (I use Crisco) (½ cup)

Directions:

1. In a small bowl, dissolve yeast in warm water. Let stand until creamy, about 5 minutes. Add buttermilk to yeast mixture, and set aside.
2. In a large bowl, combine flour, sugar, baking powder, baking soda, and salt. Cut in shortening with a pastry blender until mixture resembles coarse meal. Stir in yeast mixture until dry ingredients are moistened. Turn dough out onto a floured surface, and knead 4 or 5 times.
3. On a lightly floured surface, roll dough to ½-inch thickness. Cut out biscuits with a 2 ½-inch round cutter. Place on lightly greased baking sheets, barely touching each other. Cover, and let rise in a warm place free from drafts for 1 hour, or until almost doubled in size.
4. Preheat oven to 425°.
5. Bake for 10 to 12 minutes, or until browned.

Santa Fe Meatloaf

Ingredients:

Serves 100
(8 servings in parentheses)
- 24 eggs (2)
- 36 ounce container low sodium chicken broth (6 tablespoons)
- 36 cloves garlic (3)
- ¾ cup tomato paste (1 tablespoon)
- 8 tablespoons oregano (2 teaspoons)
- 8 tablespoons chili powder (2 teaspoons)
- salt and pepper to taste
- 24 slices high-quality whole-wheat sandwich bread, torn into 1-inch pieces (2 slices)
- 2 #10 size cans (or 11 lbs) black beans drained and rinsed (15 ounces)
- 24 pounds lean ground turkey or beef (2 pounds)
- 48 scallions, minced (4 scallions)
- 6 pounds frozen sweet corn (1 cup)
- 12 green peppers chopped fine (1 red bell pepper, chopped)
- 3 cups finely chopped cilantro (¼ cup) - not popular raw but seems to have no complaints when cooked in the meatloaf

Directions:

1. Adjust an oven rack to the middle position and heat the oven to 375°. Fold a piece of heavy-duty aluminum foil into a 10-by-6-inch rectangle, place in the center of a wire rack and place the rack on a baking sheet. Use a skewer to poke holes in the foil every ½ inch. Spray the foil with vegetable oil.
2. Whisk the eggs, broth, garlic, tomato paste, oregano, chili powder, 3 tablespoons of salt and 1 ½ tablespoons of pepper together in a large bowl. Add the bread and mash together with a rubber spatula until the mixture is uniform.

3. In a separate bowl, thoroughly mash the black beans with a potato masher until no beans are left whole. Add the mashed beans, ground beef, scallions, corn, bell pepper, cheddar and ½ the cilantro to the broth-bread mixture and combine with your hands until uniform.
4. Press the mixture together into a compact mass, then turn it out onto prepared foil on a wire rack. Press the meat to the edges of the foil into a tidy loaf 1 ½ inches high.
5. Make the glaze. Brush ½ of the glaze over the meatloaf. Bake the loaf for 20 minutes at 350°. Brush with the remaining glaze and continue to bake until the center of the loaf registers 160°, 25 to 35 minutes. Sprinkle the remaining cilantro over the meatloaf and serve.

This is not your mother's meat loaf!!

Meatloaf Glaze

Ingredients:
- 6 cups ketchup (½ cup)
- ¼ cup ground cumin powder (1 ½ teaspoons)
- 12 ounces light brown sugar (2 tablespoons)
- ½ cup Worcestershire sauce (8 tablespoons)
- ¾ cup cider vinegar (4 teaspoons)
- 1 cup minced canned chipotle chili in adobo sauce (1 ½ teaspoons)

Directions:
1. Whisk all the glaze ingredients together in a bowl until smooth.

Don't skip the glaze! It brings this ho-hum dish to new culinary height

Dropped graduation cheesecake

Cheesecake Tragedy

My sister Lauren is an interior designer, though she hasn't worked in this capacity for years. But she channels her decorating sensibilities into her entertaining. She is an incredible cook, and her food presentation is elaborate and artistic. Her artistic flair definitely came into view when she made the cheesecake centerpieces for her daughter Erica's graduation from Chatard High School in Indianapolis.

In 2002, my family lived there in a beautiful 1920s English Tudor house on historic Meridian Street. The home was situated in a two-acre park-like setting, a perfect place to host a large outside graduation gathering. So, I provided the clean and decorated house, and my sister Lauren provided all the food.

On the day of the graduation, we were all driving around town transporting food from Lauren's house to mine and getting things set up before the ceremony so that we could just open the doors to my house and be ready to entertain guests afterward. Susan, my non-foodie sister, had flown in for the event and was ready to help in any way that did not involve cooking. So, she happily offered to transport the three cheesecakes to my home from Lauren's. Lauren would arrive shortly afterwards to arrange them on a pedestal and decorate them on the dining room table. She had dipped apricots in gold and chocolate to be placed decoratively on each cake. She had made the cheesecakes in graduated sizes that would stack to create three tiers. We were all excited to witness the finished masterpiece.

Susan, already having dressed for the graduation, was unusually garbed in a flowing long skirt and new black Birkenstock-ish sandals while transporting the three boxes of cheesecakes stacked on top of each other to the extra fridge in the basement. Rushing to keep up with the busy schedule, she missed a step and turned her ankle, then fell. All three cheesecakes tumbled out of the bakery boxes and splattered on the floor. Susan, consumed with terrible guilt and in awful pain, having badly wrenched her ankle, yelled obscenities from the stairwell. Carl heard the clatter and ran down the stairs, ordering Susan not to move. He placed ice packs on her swollen ankle and began cleaning up the not insignificant mess. I had heard her scream and came running, even then realizing my priority. "Don't touch the cheesecakes," I yelled, looking to see if we could salvage anything for the party. One cake was actually still halfway in the box and could probably be carefully turned right side up and placed on a plate. At least we might save one.

As my then two-year-old daughter, Maya, sat next to Susan patting her arm and reading *Good Night Moon* in a consolatory voice, I broke the news to Lauren by phone. I could imagine her red voluminous hair flowing freely around her stunned freckled face, growing in volume as the steam escaped her ears. I suggested that I go and buy Sara Lee's frozen cheesecakes to replace the others while she and her family were at the ceremony that was now only two hours away. She flatly refused. She said she was on her way now to the grocery store and asked if she could bake the cheesecakes at my house.

This was insane, I thought. Taking a deep breath and trying not to sound too patronizing, I asked her, "Why not just buy back-up cheesecake?" There was no response on the other end. I knew that silence. It meant: You are not the boss of me, I'm your older sister, and don't give me any advice because this is how I'm going to do it no matter how insane you think I am. This was where the artist and the self-expression parts came in. We weren't just talking about feeding guests. We were talking about beauty in the form of cream cheese, graham crackers and gold dipped apricots. "OK," I said. "I will watch the cheesecakes while they bake." I was also thinking of the silver lining in not having to stand under a hot sun in eighty percent humidity at graduation. So, I stayed behind and fumed over my sister's lack of common sense, creating enough heat and humidity in my own kitchen to match that outside.

Lauren arrived in a rush ahead of the rest of the family. She came in and smiled when she saw the finished cheesecakes that were whipped together in fifteen minutes before the ceremony, now cooling in a line on the windowsill. She threw her graduation program and purse on the counter and reached down to pull out all the materials to stage the cheesecakes on the table. In those next fifteen minutes, my dining room became the most efficiently run professional catering caper you have ever witnessed. Together, we assembled tiered platforms, spread sour cream expertly to hide cracks and piped whipped cream rosettes lovingly as pillows for the dried apricots she had dipped in chocolate and gold foil. The results were stunning, and we only had time for a brief high five before the doorbell rang and Erica's celebration (right) began.

I don't know that I would have done the same, but sometimes cooking isn't really about feeding people.

The artistry of cheesecake…a family legacy

My niece Erica at her high school graduation June 2002

Rich New York-Style Cheesecake

Ingredients:

Serves 12

Crust:
- 6 ½ ounces plain cookies (graham, chocolate wafers, ginger snaps)
- 5 ½ ounces butter, melted

Filling:
- 1½ pounds cream cheese, softened
- 1 cup granulated sugar
- ¼ cup all-purpose flour
- 2 teaspoons grated lemon rind
- 4 eggs
- ⅔ cup sour cream

Directions:

To make the crust:
1. Process cookies in food processor for 15 seconds. Pour in melted butter and continue to process.
2. Press on bottom and sides of an 8-inch springform pan.

To make the filling:
1. Preheat oven to 350°.
2. Beat cheese until smooth. Add sugar, flour, rind and beat again until smooth.
3. Add eggs one at a time, then sour cream, beating after each addition.
4. Pour into prepared crust. Bake 1 hour in a water bath. Don't remove from oven when finished. Just turn off the heat and allow to cool completely in the oven.

My sister Lauren is a master cheesecake baker

Carry-On Brisket

When my oldest sister, Susan, turned fifty, her friends of thirty years rented a house on an island on Lake Champlain and threw her a weekend-long fiftieth birthday party. At the time, my other sister, Lauren, and I both lived with our families in Indianapolis and planned on attending. This was a casual event. No invitation would be coming with details. The only specifics we had were the availability of croquet and bocce equipment. Assuming that we should, as her sisters, contribute in some way to the celebration, we questioned Susan about the food for the weekend. After all, Susan grew up eating a lot of Cheese Wiz, Bugles and bologna cups; we had reason to be concerned about the food offerings. So, we asked with a mixture of enthusiastic helpfulness and slight worry how we could contribute.

Most of Susan's friends are vegetarians who can quote a lot of facts about food politics, but not all are known for their culinary talent or interest in food. Relieved to hear that the weekend would be a potluck, Lauren and I began to plan. We settled on Diane Evan's Slow-Cook Brisket, a recipe from a family friend. True, red meat was a risky venture with this crowd, but we knew that Susan loved this dish and after all, she was the birthday girl.

Lauren and I met in her kitchen to talk transport. For anyone who has ever cooked a brisket, you know that first, the meat looks really gnarly and intimidating and second, it's not a slam dunk kind of dish; it takes preparation. Given our flight would arrive an hour before the party, we had to hit the ground running with our contribution. We decided we would cook the meat before coming and warm it up for thirty minutes as soon as we arrived on the island.

The day before flying, we met and hauled up on to Lauren's butcher block counter a ten-pound slab of flesh, which took us an hour to carefully trim of fat, leaving about eight pounds of beef. We were slick with the work and stood behind a mountain of fat cubes. Then we got it into the oven with the brown sugar and soy sauce marinade and put it on for five hours. I left then. By that time, my sister had showered and was in her robe and slippers knowing that she would have to babysit the meat until it was cool enough to refrigerate.

The next morning she woke up a half hour early to lift off the fat block that forms on the surface and place the meat in doubled zip lock bags packed on ice in a red Playmate cooler. This we could carry on the plane without potential spillage or spoilage. Granted, going through security was a bit stressful. I kept worrying that at any time our sister's birthday meal could be confiscated. The idea of arriving empty-handed at our sister's fiftieth birthday potluck was not something either of us could bear. We made it all the way to Burlington without someone so much as raising an eyebrow at our cooler explanation. It made me wonder what other foods were being carried around like this in airports.

The potluck was incredible albeit eclectic. One of Susan's friends is a chef at a vegetarian restaurant. She made a ratatouille recipe that Lauren is still talking about years later. She was amazing to watch in the kitchen. Her trim figure encased in a professional white apron and her graceful, self-assured way of cooking made you realize that she was more artist than cook. I remember feeling a bit self-conscious about my own lack of culinary attire as I opened the red cooler and poured out the juice and brisket into a baking pan and popped into the oven. It could hardly be called cooking at that point. Besides ratatouille and brisket, there was Southern cornbread, marinated tofu, salads, and earthy soups, and to top it off Susan's favorite chocolate birthday cake from a local French patisserie, Mirabelles. No one needed to know how the brisket had come to be placed on the table completely cooked and steaming hot in an incredible sauce that wafted so seductively that even the vegans were salivating. Lauren and I were able to fit in just fine despite our politically incorrect offering. The story of our carry-on brisket became so hot that we found ourselves heroines of the birthday party.

Diane Evan's Brisket

Ingredients:

Serves 8 to 10
- 4 pounds brisket (already trimmed of fat), room temperature
- ½ cup dark brown sugar, packed
- ⅓ cup soy sauce
- ½ cup water
- 2 tablespoons balsamic vinegar (cooking grade)
- 1½ teaspoons fine sea salt
- ½ teaspoon coarsely ground pepper
- 1½ teaspoons garlic powder (I like Trader Joe's California garlic powder)

Directions:

1. Place brown sugar, soy sauce, water and vinegar in a small saucepan and bring to a boil, stirring until sugar is dissolved. Boil for one minute then remove from heat.
2. Rub both sides of brisket with a mixture of salt, pepper and garlic powder.
3. Place brisket in a glass rectangular pan (10 ½ by 14¾ by 2 ¼-inch Pyrex).
4. Pour sauce gently over brisket, trying to avoid washing away the dry salt/garlic mixture.
5. Cover *tightly* with foil, sealing edges well, and place in 250° oven.
6. Bake for 5 hours. Do not open the door during baking.
7. Remove and set aside to cool. Once cool enough to handle, carve beef and replace in sauce. Best left overnight in fridge. Before serving, lift off fat molecules that form on the top and then reheat at 250° in pan for 20 minutes.

Fanfare Food

Honoring people you love with a gift can be a daunting challenge. Make that gift a homemade food item and the challenge becomes even trickier. Yet, every so often, I find myself drawn by the magnetism of that challenge. So, when the president of the local food pantry where I worked announced his retirement, I knew I had to make a dessert to honor this wonderful man at his retirement fête. The level of difficulty of the dish, I felt, needed to somehow reflect the twelve-year commitment he made to the organization. In short, I wanted to honor his contribution of feeding the hungry with food.

Doing a little research, I had learned through the years, was important to pulling this off, so I called the retiring president's wife and asked what his favorite dessert was. She said, "Any kind of fruit pie." That would be a challenge, because to me, most fruit pies are visually boring. Immediately, I thought of making him a fantastic apple pie, but let's face it, apple pie is no show-stopper. It's a comfy fall dish that we all love, but it's just not that spectacular. Besides, I wanted to really sink my teeth into creating something original and magnificent; nothing ordinary would capture the profundity of his twelve-year contribution to the organization.

I looked around my kitchen and spied some beautiful purple plums that I had just picked at a local orchard. The deep purple was an absolutely regal "aha." Purple equals royalty equals president. I remembered then a dessert from my childhood, "Fruit Pizza." My sister had sent away for the "Recipe of the Month Club" after seeing an infomercial, and this was one of those fabulous dishes that my practical Depression-era mother never would have made, and my artistic sister was drawn to like a fly to sugar. I called my sister, but those recipe cards were long gone, leaving me no choice but to search the web. Eventually I found a similar recipe. The version I found would be too sweet, calling for a roll of store bought sugar cookie dough and prepared pie fillings in artificially dyed gels. So, I spent some time reworking the recipe. I started by tartening it up. The crust is basic sugar cookie dough, spread thin on a pizza pan that's been generously sprayed with cooking oil.

The cream cheese filling is fairly standard. However, I decided to change it up a little and skipped the sugar and vanilla and whipped in half a jar of lemon curd. I went to our local European import specialty shop and purchased a jar from a famous British jam and preserve company that makes a spectacular lemon curd. This resulted in a wonderful tart filling, not too sweet and lemony enough to enhance the fresh fruit without overwhelming it.

Now for the really fun and somewhat tricky part: arranging the fruit. First, you need to melt one jar of currant jam mixed with a couple tablespoons of an eau de vie (I pulled out all the stops and used Crème de Cassis). Allow the glaze to cool slightly but not enough to re-congeal; it needs to remain the consistency of syrup so that you can brush it on to the fruit. Next, I considered the color scheme I wanted to achieve and purchased fruit specifically for color. Taking my time, I sliced each fruit individually and began making my design, substituting different pieces to make sure I kept a uniform size throughout. I sliced the fruit as I needed it, instead of cutting all of it ahead of time, because I didn't want it to discolor. I brushed each slice of fruit individually with the currant jam glaze before I placed it on the crust. With the next circle of fruit, I placed the slice so it was slightly overlapped on the first circle of fruit. This gives the tart a unique three-dimensional quality much like flower petals. The final product is pretty because the glaze makes the fruit dewy.

At the party, the tart was placed on a pedestal in the middle of the table, definitely a beautiful addition and very special compared to the other items: brownies, cookies, and apple pie. I left to review my notes for the speech I was soon to give, completely forgetting about the tart.

When the formal meeting ended and the party was to begin, the retiring president was mobbed with well-wishers. He spoke informally to the crowd, thanking them for the outpouring of appreciation while people ate and toasted him.

By the time he finally reached the table with the tart, the pizza pan was empty except for a few crumbs. The guests, many of them the benefactors of his hard work with the organization, had eaten all of it. The achingly time-consuming beloved tart was no more. I felt deflated. I asked myself, "Now how will he know how much I admired him?" Honoring people with food is definitely a risky enterprise. Next time, I will deliver it to the benefactor's home, tied with satin ribbons, labeled "special delivery."

Ingredients:

Serves 12

Sugar Cookie Crust:
- 1 cup butter, softened
- ⅔ cup sugar
- 1 egg
- 1 teaspoon vanilla extract
- 2½ cups sifted all-purpose flour
- ½ teaspoon salt
- ½ teaspoon grated lemon rind

Cream Cheese Filling:
- 8 ounces softened cream cheese
- ½ cup lemon curd

Glaze and Fruit Topping:
- ½ cup currant jelly
- 1 tablespoon Crème de Cassis or other liqueur
- 1½ quarts of assorted fresh fruit slices, preferably in season with low water content (i.e. not melons)

Directions:

To make the sugar cookie crust:
1. Cream butter and sugar. Beat in egg and vanilla.
2. Stir in flour, salt, and lemon rind.
3. Chill dough for half an hour before spreading on a pizza pan lined with parchment paper.

4. Bake at 350° for 6 to 8 minutes. Best to underbake the crust. Too crispy and it might be tough to cut when you serve it.

To make the cream cheese filling:
1. Blend cream cheese and lemon curd until well incorporated.
2. Spread evenly on cooled cookie crust.

To make the glaze and fruit topping:
1. Heat currant jam to just melting and add 1 tablespoon of liqueur (optional).
2. Plan design for top of pizza. Before placing fruit on top, brush each slice individually with jam, then arrange in concentric circles, starting on the outside and moving to the center.

For the president's gift, I used nectarines on the outside rim, plums second, then strawberries and kiwis last in the center.

My father-in-law Frank preparing the baccala for Christmas Dinner

Little Italy - neighborhood bakery in Schenectady, NY where my father-in-law bought the bread when company came

The Last Supper and a Toast

(Or the Gift of Being Frank)

My father-in-law's final words were "I want food." He was offered chocolate Ensure, which was all he could handle during his final hours. Surely this was not the last supper he might have envisioned for himself and was such a stark contrast to the usual culinary abundance of home. I couldn't help shuddering when I heard this from my mother-in-law. I knew that my own relationship with food had been irrevocably altered by having broken bread with this man who presented the hearty foods of his Italian heritage each time we gathered in the kitchen.

In 1985, I met my father-in-law-to-be, Frank Calabria, at the family's Thanksgiving dinner in Schenectady, New York. That visit was my introduction to many of the family's holiday foods, like fried mozzarella in pizza dough served with syrup for a late breakfast and an unusual stuffing made of dried fruit, ground meat and brandy, which my mother-in-law referred to as "Ecuadorian filling." For this momentous first meeting with my future in-laws, I had painstakingly made homemade chocolates as my gift to Carl's family, which got set aside and no one ate. They were not part of the usual tradition. I learned then that my father-in-law loved pistachios, so when I spotted them at a farmer's market a few years later, I purchased a large quantity. Carefully packaging the red and green nuts in a canister with a homemade valentine, I sent the package from California to his home in New York. Frank never acknowledged the gift. When I called and asked if he'd received the package, he told me, "Don't waste your money on those bad nuts again." I was crestfallen. In my family book of etiquette, no one would have responded this way. They would have feigned appreciation, and I would probably have continued sending stale nuts for years to come.

In my family, you expressed love through gift giving, chosen with much "self" invested in the purchase. Homemade gifts were even more highly valued and beautifully gift-wrapped. This, too, I learned was different in Carl's family, where a check or cash was the norm. It took me several failed attempts before I got wise that food was a risky gift. Now, thirty years later, having just learned of his death, I find myself thinking about this again, seeing it from his point of view — a view that says this was a man for whom the quality of food was an everyday conversation. No one had any "self" involved. Food was always something to be critiqued — much like my French cousin, Gaby, did — Gaby was a farmer in Provence who loved discussing the flavor nuances of the olive or grape harvests. That I had taken his nut comment so personally now seems ridiculous.

As much as Frank loved food, he was no cook. Maybe it was a generational thing, for just like my father, my father-in-law's real talent was his ability to connect food and people through storytelling. The stories he told of the excellence of the sfogliatella, a flaky Italian pastry of his youth, seemed almost mythical to me. My humble offering of sfogliatella purchased in the North End of Boston didn't come close to his memory. He shook his head and said, "Not authentic." I often wondered if his use of Greek mythology to teach psychology to his students at Union College might have been used here too as a culinary standard, the heavenly pastry by which he measured my earthly offering.

Weeks after receiving the news of Frank's dismal last supper, we celebrated Frank's life by eating his favorite foods: Perreca's bread, fresh mozzarella, tomato and basil, soppressata, homemade taralles. We washed it all down with Cabernet made by Vince Sanchez, Frank's nephew by marriage. This spread was a collaborative family affair. Each person contributed to the feast, instinctively knowing where to procure the best offering for the table. The family hovered around the central island, making little bundles of bread and cheese, roasted peppers and olives and intermittently popping them into our mouths in between laughing and telling stories, and I saw Frank. He stood in front of his usual "contraband cabinet" (which held salted nuts, jellybeans and alcohol banned by his wife), toasting us with his wine glass. His white hair was carefully combed back smelling of Old Spice and he was wearing his special occasion suit jacket. He had a wide-open-mouthed laugh, his head arched back over his collar, crumbs in his beard, and was rosy-cheeked from the wine. It was not his ghost but my vivid memory. I had seen him in that exact spot for the past twenty-seven years. As a lump formed in my throat, I raised my glass to his and said, "Salute Frank!" Everyone else did the same, acknowledging that he was there with us in spirit. Clearly this was his real last supper! I found myself needing little else to eat that weekend. It seemed only the antipasti would fill the void left by Frank.

Frank not only gave me an understanding of the quality of food; he gave me much food for thought in his conversations about mindfulness, writing, creativity, psychotherapy, and life. He was such a wonderful role model about aging as I witnessed through him how to live with passion into your golden years. When I met him, he had just retired as a psychology professor from Union College but continued his psychotherapy practice. He wrote two books during his retirement and loved to talk about his work, but he always asked me with sincere interest what was going on in my life. He was a lifelong student, never missing the opportunity to hear about a new paradigm of thinking. In recent years, we suggested books to each other and then discussed books like *The Art of Possibility* by Rosamund and Benjamin Zander. He would comment on what changes he was making in his life based on the inspiration from his reading and I would share my own. This candid talk about creativity, positivity and universal truths was a rare phenomenon for me at the time. While being at home raising young children, his spark of intellectual stimulation momentarily helped sate my hunger for meaningful discourse.

Calabria Antipasti

Ingredients:

Serves 6 to 8
- 1 jar oil-cured olives
- 1 tin smoked oysters
- 1 jar roasted red peppers
- 2 small, sliced tomatoes with fresh basil
- ½ pound fresh mozzarella
- 1 loaf thick and crusty Italian Bread (like Perrecca's in Schenectady, NY)
- fresh salted nuts (almonds and pistachios)
- cheeses, assorted from an Italian deli
- soppressata (best from an Italian deli — if made in Calabria, tends to be spicy)

Directions:

1. Place olives, oysters and red peppers in their own ceramic bowls so that their liquids remain separate and can later be returned to the refrigerator.
2. Place the sliced tomatoes on a wooden cutting board with the mozzarella and fresh basil so that picking up each and placing it on a slice of bread is easy.
3. Extra cheeses should be on a different cutting board, perhaps shared with the sliced soppressata if space is an issue. The final antipasti will have a colorful, inviting look, drawing the family to stand around the arrangement, admire and graze while catching up on family stories.

The assorted ingredients do not all have to be served at the same time, though they could be if it's a large gathering.

Taralli with Anise

Ingredients:
Makes a grocery bag full!
*Caution: this recipe takes a full afternoon to execute.
- 6 eggs (room temperature)
- 1/2 package dry yeast (dissolved in 1/2 cup lukewarm water)
- 1 additional cup water
- 4 tablespoons butter, melted
- 1/4 cup vegetable oil
- 1.5 tablespoons salt
- 1 tablespoon anise seeds
- 2 teaspoons of ground black pepper (optional)
- 2.5 pounds unbleached white flour
- 1 tablespoons salt for the water used to boil the taralli

Directions:
1. In a large bowl, lightly beat eggs with salt.
2. Add melted butter and oil.
3. Add diluted yeast solution PLUS the additional 1 cup warm water.
4. Gradually, add ¾ of the flour to liquid mixture and mix until thickened and ready to knead using the KitchenAid mixer with beaters.
5. Change to using the dough hook attachment when dough begins to form and is thick enough to knead. Sprinkle on top of the dough the anise seeds and incorporate the remaining ¼ of flour and an additional 1 cup of warm water.
6. Turn dough out on a floured surface and knead dough until smooth (if not using a mixer with dough hook).
7. Oil a large bowl in which to place the dough. Spread oil on top of dough, lightly. Put waxed paper on top, then towels or blanket. Put in warm place (with no drafts) to rise, for 1 hour.
8. Fill large pot ¾ full with water and add 1 tablespoon salt. Bring to a boil.

9. Preheat oven to 375°. (Use convection oven if you have one.)
10. After dough rises, remove dough and divide into 3 parts. Roll out one piece on a lightly floured surface to approximately 7" wide and 18" long. Cut 7" strips ½" width and form into knots or horshoes and place on a lightly oiled cookie sheet. Repeat with each dough ball until all tarallis are formed.
11. Place 10-15 tarralis in boiling water. When they rise to top, cook for 2 to 3 minutes more and then remove with a slotted spoon then place on a wire rack positioned inside a cookie sheet.
12. Bake in oven until golden brown, about 20-25 minutes. Check closely and rotate pans half-way thru baking.
13. 14. Let cool on racks or granite surface.

A Toast Inspired by Frank:

May you taste the difference between a stale and fresh pistachio; May your kitchen be overflowing with good wine and crusty bread; May you delight in the aroma of homemade sauce and appreciate the love of the family united at your table. Salute!

When and how to eat a tarallo is really very important to its overall enjoyment. These traditional Easter baked goods are somewhere between a pretzel and a cookie. The recipe I offer is the "savory" one. It is best when accompanied by a glass of wine and served with the antipasti, though there is a sweet version that is best dunked in coffee at the end of a meal. I saw Frank dunk this one into both his wine and his coffee—and only when there was company in the house. The importance is that they are served with a beverage that complements the dryness of the texture.

Ingredients:

Serves a large Italian family
- 1 package dry quick-rise yeast
- 1⅓ cups 85° water
- 4 cups all-purpose flour
- 2 tablespoons olive oil
- 1 teaspoon salt
- ¼ to ½ cup honey (liquid)
- 1 (2 ounce) container colored sprinkles (nonpareil, optional)

Directions:

1. Dissolve yeast in warm water in a large glass measuring cup. Mix in salt after yeast is dissolved to protect the integrity of the yeast. Let stand for 5 minutes to activate.
2. Pour yeast mixture into stand mixer's metal bowl.
3. Add 1 tablespoon of the olive oil and mix in 2 ½ cups of the flour with the paddle attachment.
4. Once the dough gathers into one ball, change the paddle to the dough hook. If it's still too sticky to form one mass, keep adding a little flour until the dough can be kneaded with the hook.
5. Knead the dough with the dough hook for 5 minutes until all the flour is incorporated and the dough is still soft and easy to handle.
6. Turn the dough out on the counter while you wash and prepare the metal bowl for the dough to rise in. Use the remaining 1 tablespoon of olive oil to grease the interior of the metal bowl and place the dough back in the bowl, turning it over so all sides are well-greased.
7. Cover and place bowl in a warm place to rise for 1 to 3 hours. (I usually use the lid that comes with my stand mixer and place it in an oven warmed at the lowest temperature — turning it off once I place the dough inside.)

8. Once dough has risen to twice its original size, place on the counter to begin making the zeppoles. Divide the dough into 8 sections. Roll out each section so that it forms a long snake of dough approximately 1 inch in diameter. Using a sharp knife or dough cutter, cut off 2-inch pieces of dough and roll on a lightly floured counter to form a small 1 ½ to 2-inch balls.
9. Meanwhile, heat oil in an electric fryer or deep saucepan until reaches 350°. Once the oil is hot, drop in a handful of dough balls and watch carefully, turning them with a slotted spoon so that all sides become golden brown — don't over fry.
10. Working in batches, remove the fried zeppoles from the hot oil and place on a brown paper bag lining a cookie sheet to drain excess oil.
11. Once drained, place zeppoles in a large ceramic serving bowl. After each batch of hot zeppoles are placed in the bowl, drizzle with honey and stir the zeppoles so that they are well covered. Colored sprinkles can be added per your family's preference.

Zeppoles are a fun Calabria Christmas Eve tradition. I usually mix the dough up and let it rise while we attend Christmas Eve service. Once we return from church, we all put on our comfy pajamas and congregate around the kitchen counter to make the zeppoles together, each person taking up a different part of the assembly line work. Kyle particularly loves cooking the dough especially when he's wearing a Santa hat. By the end of the evening, there are usually few zeppoles remaining in the bowl as everyone does some sampling throughout the process. Though traditions come and go, this is one that I believe will live on in my children's households in the years to come.

Christmas Morning Popovers

Ingredients:

Serves 12
- 3½ cups of whole milk, warmed
- 4 cups of bread flour
- 1½ teaspoons salt
- 1 teaspoon baking soda
- 6 large eggs, room temperature
- 4 tablespoons of melted, unsalted butter

Directions:

1. Place the milk in a bowl or use a 4 cup glass measuring cup and microwave on high for approximately 1 ½ minutes, or until warm to the touch.
2. Spoon the flour into a cup and level it off with a knife. Do not shake the cup to settle the flour.
3. In a large bowl, sift the flour, salt, and baking powder together and set aside.
4. In a blender combine the eggs, milk, melted butter; then dump out approximately half the milk/egg mixture in a separate large bowl. In batches, process approximately 10 seconds until each ½ is blended.
5. Add ½ the flour mixture to half the egg/milk mixture in the blender and process for 10-15 seconds. Do not overmix. Scrape down the sides of the blender with a rubber spatula if necessary. Repeat with the other half of the ingredients — ending with combining all in a large bowl. Allow to rest for 60 minutes — do not refrigerate the batter!
6. Preheat the oven to 450°. Place the oven rack on the middle rung and heat the empty popover pan for 5 minutes, or until it is hot. Once the oven is the correct temperature and the empty popover pan is hot, quickly remove the popover pan from the oven; lightly spray the popover pan with a nonstick spray — very thin coat.

7. Fill the popover cups almost to the top with the batter. If you leave one of the cups in the pan empty, fill it half full of water to protect the pan from the high heat. Immediately place the pan back into the hot oven and back at 450° for 15 minutes.
8. Without opening the oven, reduce the temperature to 375° and bake for another 20-25 minutes or until deep golden brown on the outside and airy on the inside. Underbaking can cause popovers to collapse after they're removed from the oven.
9. Remove popovers from the oven and unmold onto a rack. Pierce the sides with the tip of a sharp knife to let steam escape (this will keep the exterior crisp, the interior moist, and prevent the popovers from collapsing).

Resist the urge to open the oven door. If you open the oven door, the heat escapes, the oven cools down, the steam inside the popovers condenses and the popovers collapse.

Serve immediately with lots of butter, jam, honey, syrup, and wonderful fillings.

End of Garden Soup

About the third week of September, I begin to suffer from a gardener's slump. By then I've lost my vernal vim and vigor. Yet the garden is still producing and beckoning me to harvest the rewards of my summer's toil. September is a transitional month when the outside still requires attention and all the school year's academic and sports programs draw me inside as they make demands on my calendar. This is the time to simplify both my gardening and cooking.

I look around my kitchen and see all those baskets of tomatoes, peppers and eggplants beginning to sink from robust health. If we don't eat them soon, it will be too late. The idea of chopping, peeling, and processing them is too daunting. But as the air begins to chill and I begin to crave soup, End of Garden Soup solves this problem of preparing all the late harvest vegetables with minimal effort.

I love this soup for its ease, but just as much for the incredible aroma it has as all the veggies roast in the oven. The melding of fresh herbs, buttery olive oil, tangy tomatoes and piquant peppers makes this soup a repeat command performance year after year. Even my husband asks for seconds as I have deceptively omitted the word "eggplant" in the description.

This dish pays tribute to the last of summer's treasures. Nothing could be easier than generously dousing my roaster with olive oil, pricking all the veggies with a fork, and tossing them in with a whole bulb of fresh garlic. After roasting in a hot oven for an hour, simply scrape away the peels and seeds and pour all the pulp and juices into your food processor and puree. Place in a saucepan with chicken or vegetable broth and whisk and heat. Season with fresh thyme, oregano, balsamic vinegar, salt and pepper. Serve with croutons and freshly grated parmesan.

When I slow down enough to enjoy the last hoorah of autumn, I wonder at my dahlias' riotous colors, like fireworks marking the end of the season. I try to immerse myself in this warmth and wonder by picking peppers and tomatoes and eggplants — I just have to bring their saturated colors into the kitchen. Each year, when I create this soup, I am part of generations past who come alive in the kitchen. The recipes sustain me through the seasons of my life. They bring me back each year to End of Garden Soup and the wonder of the taste of stories.

End of Garden Soup

Ingredients:

Serves 6

- 1 to 2 eggplants, quartered lengthwise (about a pound to a pound and a half)
- ½ head garlic, top cut off for easy access
- 3 pounds tomatoes, halved
- 1 large onion, quartered
- 1 whole red bell pepper, halved and seeded
- ⅓ cup olive oil
- salt and pepper to taste
- 6 cups chicken stock, homemade preferable
- 2 tablespoons balsamic vinegar
- 2 teaspoons fresh basil
- 2 teaspoons fresh oregano, finely chopped
- 2 teaspoons fresh thyme, finely chopped

Directions:

1. Preheat the oven to 450°.
2. Place all veggies in a large roaster, attempting to make one single layer. Drizzle olive oil over veggies and bake, uncovered 30 to 45 minutes until they are soft with brown edges.
3. Cool eggplant, then scrape flesh from skin into a food processor fitted with a metal blade; discard skin.
4. Remove garlic and onion from their skins and add to the food processor. Add remaining roasted veggies and accumulated juices from the bottom of the pan to the food processor and puree until smooth.
5. Pour puree into a large saucepan and stir in stock, vinegar and fresh herbs. Heat soup until it simmers gently.
6. Serve in soup bowls with freshly grated Parmesan cheese and homemade croutons.

Acknowledgments
I am so thankful for....

My husband's patience, encouragement, and amazing photographic skills. His insatiable desire to travel and his thirst for adventure giving me a lifetime of diverse and unique culinary experiences to draw upon. But most of all for being the keeper of my heart.

My mother, who encouraged me to cook and experiment and never waste a thing. My father, for great story-telling and making sure that I knew an entirely different world existed outside my hometown. My sisters, Lauren and Susan, for helping me piece together the past so that I could represent it here as accurately as possible and for their encouragement of the project. Reminding me that sometimes a little exaggeration makes for a better story!

My kids: Kyle, Nico and Maya — for inspiration for many of these stories. Thank you for being "good guinea pigs." I hope you will take the culinary torch and pass it on. And to you Maya for getting me to the finish line.

My mother-in-law, Angela Calabria, who always welcomed my help in her kitchen and was the first to offer help in mine. To my sister-in-law, Marie, and brother-in-law, Mark, who have been excellent kindred kitchen spirits. I so appreciate our shared passion for high-quality, healthy, simple food.

My good friend Maile Hulihan, who is really my spirit sister — thank you for taking all my impromptu calls, and acting as a sounding board offering patient, wise counsel for the next steps of my book and for being honest about when I needed to dig deeper and persevere. My dear friend Kris Earle, who is an amazing cook and ally — thank you for a lifetime of cooking adventures and all your support of this project. You are always with me even when we live far away.

Barbara Blankenship, who inspired me to take my cooking to the masses and who shares my enjoyment of "scarcity" cooking. My writer's group, for listening, critiquing, and encouraging me every step of the way. I would have abandoned this project long ago if it weren't for your input. I literally wouldn't have written this without you. Liz Stasior and her beautiful sense of design and sweet encouraging way of helping me complete the final phase of this project.

My 50th birthday party attendees, for cooking all my recipes for a potluck and then providing helpful feedback from the experience.

All those people I've cooked with. The synergy found while cooking shoulder to shoulder has made for the happiest times of my life.

www.ingramcontent.com/pod-product-compliance
Lightning Source LLC
Chambersburg PA
CBHW061128170426
43209CB00014B/1701